UNIX FOR DUMMIES®

Quick Reference

2nd Edition

by Margaret Levine Young and John R. Levine

IDG BOOKS WORLDWIDE

IDG Books Worldwide, Inc.
An International Data Group Company

Foster City, CA ✦ Chicago, IL ✦ Indianapolis, IN ✦ Braintree, MA ✦ Southlake, TX

UNIX For Dummies® Quick Reference, 2nd Edition

Published by
IDG Books Worldwide, Inc.
An International Data Group Company
919 E. Hillsdale Blvd.
Suite 400
Foster City, CA 94404

Library of Congress Catalog Card No.: 95-81093

ISBN: 1-56884-979-6

Printed in the United States of America

10 9 8 7 6 5 4 3 2

2A/RQ/RR/ZV/IN

Distributed in the United States by IDG Books Worldwide, Inc.

Distributed by Macmillan Canada for Canada; by Computer and Technical Books for the Caribbean Basin; by Contemporanea de Ediciones for Venezuela; by Distribuidora Cuspide for Argentina; by CITEC for Brazil; by Ediciones ZETA S.C.R. Ltda. for Peru; by Editorial Limusa SA for Mexico; by Transworld Publishers Limited in the United Kingdom and Europe; by Al-Maiman Publishers & Distributors for Saudi Arabia; by Simron Pty. Ltd. for South Africa; by IDG Communications (HK) Ltd. for Hong Kong; by Toppan Company Ltd. for Japan; by Addison Wesley Publishing Company for Korea; by Longman Singapore Publishers Ltd. for Singapore, Malaysia, Thailand, and Indonesia; by Unalis Corporation for Taiwan; by WS Computer Publishing Company, Inc. for the Philippines; by WoodsLane Pty. Ltd. for Australia; by WoodsLane Enterprises Ltd. for New Zealand.

For general information on IDG Books Worldwide's books in the U.S., please call our Consumer Customer Service department at 800-762-2974. For reseller information, including discounts and premium sales, please call our Reseller Customer Service department at 800-434-3422.

For information on where to purchase IDG Books Worldwide's books outside the U.S., contact IDG Books Worldwide at 415-655-3021 or fax 415-655-3295.

For information on translations, contact Marc Jeffrey Mikulich, Director, Foreign & Subsidiary Rights, at IDG Books Worldwide, 415-655-3018 or fax 415-655-3295.

For sales inquiries and special prices for bulk quantities, write to the address above or call IDG Books Worldwide at 415-655-3200.

For information on using IDG Books Worldwide's books in the classroom, or ordering examination copies, contact the Education Office at 800-434-2086 or fax 817-251-8174.

For authorization to photocopy items for corporate, personal, or educational use, please contact Copyright Clearance Center, 222 Rosewood Drive, Danvers, MA 01923, or fax 508-750-4470.

is a trademark under exclusive license to IDG Books Worldwide, Inc., from International Data Group, Inc.

About the Authors

John Levine and Margaret Levine Young were members of a computer club in high school (this was before high school students, or even high schools, had computers). They came in contact with Theodor H. Nelson, the author of *Computer Lib* and the inventor of hypertext, who fostered the idea that computers should not be taken seriously. He showed them that everyone can understand and use computers.

John wrote his first program in 1967 on an IBM 1130 (a computer roughly as powerful as your typical modern digital wristwatch — only more difficult to use). His first exposure to UNIX was while hanging out with friends in Princeton in 1974; he became an official UNIX system administrator at Yale in 1975. John began working part-time for Interactive Systems, the first commercial UNIX company, in 1977 and has been in and out of the UNIX biz ever since. He used to spend most of his time writing software, but now he mostly writes books because it's more fun. He also teaches some computer courses and publishes and edits an incredibly technoid magazine called *The Journal of C Language Translation*. He has a B.A. and a Ph.D. in computer science from Yale University.

Margy has been using small computers since the 1970s. She graduated from UNIX on a PDP/11 to Apple DOS on an Apple II to MS-DOS and UNIX on a variety of machines. She has done all kinds of jobs that involve explaining to people that computers aren't as mysterious as they might think, including managing the use of PCs at Columbia Pictures, teaching scientists and engineers what computers are good for, and writing computer manuals. She has been president of NYUPC, the New York PC Users Group. Margy has written several computer books, including *Understanding Javelin PLUS* (John also wrote part of it) and *The Complete Guide to PC-File*. She has a degree in computer science from Yale University.

ABOUT IDG BOOKS WORLDWIDE

Welcome to the world of IDG Books Worldwide.

IDG Books Worldwide, Inc., is a subsidiary of International Data Group, the world's largest publisher of computer-related information and the leading global provider of information services on information technology. IDG was founded more than 25 years ago and now employs more than 7,700 people worldwide. IDG publishes more than 250 computer publications in 67 countries (see listing below). More than 70 million people read one or more IDG publications each month.

Launched in 1990, IDG Books Worldwide is today the #1 publisher of best-selling computer books in the United States. We are proud to have received 8 awards from the Computer Press Association in recognition of editorial excellence and three from Computer Currents' First Annual Readers' Choice Awards, and our best-selling ...For Dummies® series has more than 19 million copies in print with translations in 28 languages. IDG Books Worldwide, through a joint venture with IDG's Hi-Tech Beijing, became the first U.S. publisher to publish a computer book in the People's Republic of China. In record time, IDG Books Worldwide has become the first choice for millions of readers around the world who want to learn how to better manage their businesses.

Our mission is simple: Every one of our books is designed to bring extra value and skill-building instructions to the reader. Our books are written by experts who understand and care about our readers. The knowledge base of our editorial staff comes from years of experience in publishing, education, and journalism — experience which we use to produce books for the '90s. In short, we care about books, so we attract the best people. We devote special attention to details such as audience, interior design, use of icons, and illustrations. And because we use an efficient process of authoring, editing, and desktop publishing our books electronically, we can spend more time ensuring superior content and spend less time on the technicalities of making books.

You can count on our commitment to deliver high-quality books at competitive prices on topics you want to read about. At IDG Books Worldwide, we continue in the IDG tradition of delivering quality for more than 25 years. You'll find no better book on a subject than one from IDG Books Worldwide.

WINNER
Eighth Annual
Computer Press
Awards ≥ 1992

WINNER
Ninth Annual
Computer Press
Awards ≥ 1993

John J. Kilcullen

John Kilcullen
President and CEO
IDG Books Worldwide, Inc.

IDG BOOKS WORLDWIDE

IDG Books Worldwide, Inc., is a subsidiary of International Data Group, the world's largest publisher of computer-related information and the leading global provider of information services on information technology. International Data Group publishes over 250 computer publications in 67 countries. Seventy million people read one or more International Data Group publications each month. International Data Group's publications include: ARGENTINA: Computerworld Argentina, GamePro, Infoworld, PC World Argentina; AUSTRALIA: Australian Macworld, Client/Server Journal, Computer Living, Computerworld, Digital News, Network World, PC World, Publishing Essentials, Reseller; AUSTRIA: Computerwelt, PC TEST; BELARUS: PC World Belarus; BELGIUM: Data News; BRAZIL: Annuário de Informática, Computerworld Brazil, Connections, Super Game Power, Macworld, PC World Brazil, Publish Brazil, SUPERGAME; BULGARIA: Computerworld Bulgaria, Networkworld/Bulgaria, PC & MacWorld Bulgaria; CANADA: CIO Canada, ComputerWorld Canada, InfoCanada, Network World Canada, Reseller World; CHILE: Computerworld Chile, GamePro, PC World Chile; COLUMBIA: Computerworld Colombia, GamePro, PC World Colombia; COSTA RICA: PC World Costa Rica/Nicaragua; THE CZECH AND SLOVAK REPUBLICS: Computerworld Czechoslovakia, Elektronika Czechoslovakia, PC World Czechoslovakia; DENMARK: Communications World, Computerworld Danmark, Macworld Danmark, PC World Danmark, PC World Danmark Supplements, TECH World; DOMINICAN REPUBLIC: PC World Republica Dominicana; ECUADOR: PC World Ecuador, GamePro; EGYPT: Computerworld Middle East, PC World Middle East; EL SALVADOR: PC World Centro America; FINLAND: MikroPC, Tietoverkko, Tietoviikko; FRANCE: Distributique, Golden, Info PC, Le Guide du Monde Informatique, Le Monde Informatique, Reseaux & Telecoms; GERMANY: Computer Business, Computerwoche, Computerwoche Extra, Computerwoche Focus, Electronic Entertainment, GamePro, I/M Information Management, Macwelt, PC Welt; GREECE: GamePro, Macworld & Publish; GUATEMALA: PC World Centro America; HONDURAS: PC World Centro America; HONG KONG: Computerworld Hong Kong, PCWorld Hong Kong, Publish in Asia; HUNGARY: ABCD CD-ROM, Computerworld Szamitastechnika, PC & Mac World Hungary, PC-X Magazine; INDIA: Computerworld India, PC World India, Publish in Asia; INDONESIA: InfoKomputer PC World, Komputek Computerworld, Publish in Asia; IRELAND: ComputerScope, PC Live!; ISRAEL: PC World 32 BIT, People & Computers; ITALY: Computerworld Italia, Computerworld Italia Special Editions, Lotus Italia, Macworld Italia, Networking Italia, PC Shopping, PC World Italia, PC World/Walt Disney; JAPAN: Macworld Japan, Nikkei Personal Computing, SunWorld Japan, Windows World Japan; KENYA: East African Computer News; KOREA: Hi-Tech Information/Computerworld, Macworld Korea, PC World Korea; MACEDONIA: PC World Macedonia; MALAYSIA: Computerworld Malaysia, PC World Malaysia, Publish in Asia; MEXICO: Computerworld Mexico, GamePro, Macworld, PC World Mexico; MYANMAR: PC World Myanmar; NETHERLANDS: Computable, Computer! Totaal, LAN Magazine, Macworld, Net Magazine; NEW ZEALAND: Computer Buyer, Computerworld New Zealand, MTB, Network World, PC World New Zealand; NICARAGUA: PC World Costa Rica/Nicaragua; NIGERIA: PC World Africa; NORWAY: Computerworld Norge, Computerworld Privat, CW Rapport Klient/Tjener, CW Rapport Nettverk & Telecom, CW Rapport Offentlig Sektor, IDG's KURSGUIDE, Macworld Norge, Multimedia World, PC World Ekspress, PC World Nettverk, PC World Norge, PC World's Produktguide, Windows Spesial; PAKISTAN: Computerworld Pakistan, PC World Pakistan; PANAMA: GamePro, PC World Panama; PARAGUAY: PC World Paraguay; P. R. OF CHINA: China Computerworld, China Infoworld, Computer for Communication, Electronic Product World, Electronics Today, Game Camp, PC World China, Popular Computer Week, Software World, Telecom Product World; PERU: Computerworld Peru, GamePro, PC World Profesional Peru, PC World Peru; POLAND: Computerworld Poland, Computerworld Special Report, Macworld, Networld, PC World Komputer; PHILIPPINES: Computerworld Philippines, PC Digest, Publish in Asia; PORTUGAL: Cerebro/PC World, Correio Informático/Computerworld, Mac•In/PC•In Portugal; PUERTO RICO: PC World Puerto Rico; ROMANIA: Computerworld Romania, PC World Romania, Telecom Romania; RUSSIA: Computerworld Rossiya, Network World Russia, PC World Russia; SINGAPORE: Computerworld Singapore, PC World Singapore, Publish in Asia; SLOVENIA: MONITOR; SOUTH AFRICA: Computing S.A., Network World S.A., Software World; SPAIN: Computerworld España, COMUNICACIONES WORLD, Dealer World, Macworld España, PC World España; SWEDEN: CAP&Design, Computer Sweden, Corporate Computing, MacWorld, Maxi Data, MikroDatorn, Nätverk & Kommunikation, PC/Aktiv, PC World, Windows World; SWITZERLAND: Computerworld Schweiz, Macworld Schweiz, PCtip; TAIWAN: Computerworld Taiwan, Macworld Taiwan, PC World Taiwan, Publish Taiwan, Windows World; THAILAND: Thai Computerworld, Publish in Asia; TURKEY: Computerworld Monitör, MACWORLD Turkiye, PC WORLD Turkiye; UKRAINE: Computerworld Kiev, Computers & Software Magazine, PC World Ukraine; UNITED KINGDOM: Acorn User, Amiga Action, Amiga Computing, Amiga, Appletalk, CD Powerplay, CD-ROM Now, Computing, Connexion, GamePro, Lotus Magazine, Macaction, Macworld, PC Home, PC Answers, PC Today, Parents and Computers, PC Home, PC Works, The WEB; UNITED STATES: Cable in the Classroom, CD Review, CIO Magazine, Computerworld, Computerworld Client/Server Journal, Digital Video Magazine, DOS World, Electronic, InfoWorld, I-Way, Macworld, Maximize, MULTIMEDIA WORLD, Network World, PC World, PUBLISH, SWATPro Magazine, Video Event, WebMaster; URUGUAY: PC World Uruguay; VENEZUELA: Computerworld Venezuela, GamePro, PC World Venezuela; and VIETNAM: PC World Vietnam   10/17/95

Acknowledgments

The authors would like to thank Allan Davis, Jordan Young, Lydia Spitzer, Meg Young, Steve Emmerich, and the entire gang at Lexington Playcare Center (especially Cate, Rachel, Bridget, Terri, and Chris) for their support in writing this book. We also want to acknowledge Pam Mourouzis, Tammy Castleman, Kelly Ewing, and Becky Whitney for their fine editing and Barb Potter for her fine proofreading eye.

(The Publisher would like to give special thanks to Patrick J. McGovern, without whom this book would not have been possible.)

Credits

**Senior Vice President
and Publisher**
Milissa L. Koloski

Associate Publisher
Diane Graves Steele

Brand Manager
Judith A. Taylor

Editorial Managers
Kristin A. Cocks
Mary Corder

Product Development Manager
Mary Bednarek

Editorial Executive Assistant
Richard Graves

Editorial Assistants
Constance Carlisle
Chris Collins
Kevin Spencer

Production Director
Beth Jenkins

Production Assistant
Jacalyn L. Pennywell

**Supervisor of
Project Coordination**
Cindy L. Phipps

Supervisor of Page Layout
Kathie S. Schnorr

**Supervisor of Graphics and
Design**
Shelley Lea

Reprint Coordination
Tony Augsburger
Theresa Sánchez-Baker
Todd Klemme

Blueline Coordinator
Patricia R. Reynolds

Media/Archive Coordination
Leslie Popplewell
Melissa Stauffer
Jason Marcuson

Project Editors
Pamela Mourouzis
Rebecca Whitney

Editors
Tamara S. Castleman
Kelly Ewing

Technical Reviewer
S.E. Potter-Newsome

Project Coordinator
J. Tyler Connor

Graphics Coordination
Gina Scott
Angela F. Hunckler
Carla Radzikinas

Production Page Layout
Cameron Booker
Linda M. Boyer
Maridee V. Ennis
Jill Lyttle
Mark C. Owens

Proofreaders
Barb Potter
Gwenette Gaddis
Christine Meloy Beck
Dwight Ramsey
Carl Saff
Robert Springer

Indexer
Sharon Hilgenberg

Cover Design
Kavish + Kavish

Table of Contents

Part IV: Using Text Editors (ed, vi, emacs, and pico) 111

Part V: Sending and Receiving Electronic Mail 123

Part VI: Connecting to Other Computers 139

How to Use This Book

At last, a UNIX reference book that includes only the tasks and commands you might conceivably have some interest in! In this book, you will find information about lots of UNIX commands — more than 100 — and how to use them, but we have left out the other 10 zillion commands and options that only nerds love.

We have also included information about several widely used parts of UNIX: the Motif window manager; the ed, vi, emacs, and pico text editors; electronic mail; and networking. Don't flip through lots of confusing manuals to find that command you are looking for — just check out the relevant part of this book. The table of contents and the extensive index should help you find whatever you need.

Finding Things in This Book

This book is divided into eight sections so that you can find things fast.

Part I, "Getting to Know the Shell," has information about how to type commands, name files and directories, and use pipes and filters.

Part II, "UNIX Commands," contains our favorite 100 or so UNIX commands, with the options you are likely to use. We have included examples and warnings when necessary.

Part III, "Using Motif," was written for people who use UNIX's most popular window manager.

Part IV, "Using Text Editors (ed, vi, emacs, and pico)," contains command summaries for these four editors.

Part V, "Sending and Receiving Electronic Mail," has instructions for using the elm and Mail programs to handle your electronic mail.

Part VI, "Connecting to Other Computers," contains commands for accessing computers on a network.

Part VII, "Finding Resources on the Net," contains instructions for finding information on networks, including the Internet.

And Part VIII, "Usenet Newsgroups," describes Usenet, the global networked bulletin board system.

There is also a glossary at the end of the book that you can use to look up the terms that you have forgotten or that are just plain baffling to you.

Conventions Used in This Book

When you have to type something, it appears in boldface, like this: type **elm**. When we want you to type something longer, it appears like this:

```
terribly important UNIX command
```

Be sure to type it just as it appears. Use the same capitalization we do because UNIX considers the capital and small versions of the same letter to be totally different beasts. Then press the Enter or Return key.

In the text, UNIX commands and filenames are shown `in this typeface`.

Part II contains a cryptic "UNIXspeak" version of each command that shows all its options and arguments. Information in **boldface** is required when you're using the command. Stuff in [square brackets] is optional, so try leaving it out. Text in *italics* represents information that you provide; if you see *filename,* for example, fill in the name of the file you want to work with. Don't worry; we explain it all later.

The Cast of Icons

For each command or task that we describe — and whenever we provide other important information — we include icons that tell you about what you are reading.

A tip that can save you time or impress your local UNIX guru.

This icon points out the lightning-fast way to do something.

Watch out! Something about this command or task can make trouble for you.

Who knows why, but this command or task may not work as you would typically expect.

An extra-neat trick or feature.

A command or task that is useful if your computer is connected to a network. If not, don't use it!

A handy cross-reference to the chapters in *UNIX For Dummies,* 2nd Edition and other related *...For Dummies* books that cover this topic in more detail.

Getting to Know the Shell

We work from the outside in, so the shell sounds like a good place to begin. (If this statement makes you think that UNIX resembles an insect, only not as attractive, then we think along the same lines.) The *shell* program reads your commands and processes them.

There are several shells, the most popular of which are Bourne, C, BASH, and Korn, which are described in this part. Some of these shells have extra commands that the others don't, and the syntax of the commands may differ slightly between shells, but they all act essentially the same.

Unless you're the victim — er, beneficiary — of a fancy graphical interface, the only way to communicate with UNIX is to type commands. Here, we discuss what commands look like and some general rules that apply to all commands. Even if you have a graphical interface, you will end up typing shell commands into a window, so you'll need some of this information anyway.

See Part III for more information about Motif, the most popular graphical interface.

In this part...

- ✔ Entering commands
- ✔ Understanding how information is organized in files and directories
- ✔ Using wildcard characters to specify files you want to process
- ✔ Determining which shell you are using
- ✔ Getting help

Directories

A *directory* is a special kind of file that contains the names of other files. All files are arranged in directories.

At any given moment, one directory is your *current directory* (or *working directory*) of files you are using right now. When you first log in, your current directory is your *home directory* (or *login directory*), which the system administrator made for you.

You can — and usually should — make other directories in which to store files for various projects. You can switch to other directories with the cd command, make new directories with mkdir, and get rid of directories you no longer want with rmdir. (*See* the entries for these commands in Part II.)

✦ In the C, BASH, and Korn shells, the ~ (tilde) is shorthand for your home directory. For example, if your home directory is /usr/elvis, then ~/hits is the same as /usr/elvis/hits.

✦ As with filenames, you can use uppercase and lowercase letters, digits, periods, and underscores in your directory names. UNIX considers uppercase and lowercase different.

A good rule of thumb is to use all lowercase for files and initial capital letters for directories.

Filenames

Information that you save is stored in files. Each file has a name (actually, each file can have many names — *see* the ln entry in Part II). You can use letters, digits, periods, hyphens, and underscores in filenames. (You can use other characters as well, but stick to these to avoid confusion.) Uppercase and lowercase are different, so tadpole, TadPole, and TADPOLE are different names.

Don't use odd characters in filenames, such as: / ! @ # $ ^ & * - ( ) + ' " \ | ? Also, don't use spaces in filenames. Most programs won't let you anyway. Use periods or underlines to string words together, like this:

pumpkin_soup_recipe

Finding Out Which Shell You're Using

Here's a handy way to find out which shell you're using. Type the following line:

echo $RANDOM

and then press the Enter key. If you get a blank line, it's the *Bourne shell*. If you get the following line:

```
RANDOM: Undefined variable
```

it's the *C shell*. If you get a five-digit random number, it's the *Korn shell* (*ksh*) or *BASH*. To tell ksh from BASH, type

```
help
```

If you get a page of command descriptions, you have BASH. If not, you've got the Korn shell.

Getting Help by Using man

If you need help with a UNIX command, you can display the online reference manual by using the man (for *manual*) command. Simply type **man**, followed by the name of the command you need information about.

If you have forgotten the options that you can use with the ls command, for example, type this:

```
man ls
```

On some systems, the manual page flies by too fast to read. You can force it to display a page at a time by running the output through the more command. Type this:

```
man ls | more
```

See also *UNIX For Dummies,* 2nd Edition (IDG Books Worldwide, Inc.). More detailed information about shells and commands can be found in Chapter 2 and about files and directories in Chapters 5 and 6. Chapter 7 of *MORE UNIX For Dummies* (IDG Books Worldwide, Inc.) covers startup commands.

Pathnames

A *pathname* tells UNIX how to find the particular file you want. If you use a plain filename (tadpole, for example), UNIX understands it as a file in the current directory. You refer to files in other directories by using a list of names strung together with slashes. Typing the name **snacks/tadpole** tells UNIX to look in the current directory for a subdirectory called snacks and to look there for a file called tadpole.

If the path begins with a slash, it's an *absolute path,* or one that starts from the "root" of the file system. A typical absolute path is /usr/elvis/songs/hound_dog. An absolute path always means the same thing, regardless of what your current directory is.

Quoting Characters on the Command Line

Sometimes you have to use special characters in your commands. For example, to list filenames that have a question mark in them, you need to tell the shell that the question mark you are typing should *not* be interpreted as a wildcard character. This is called *quoting* the character.

To quote any special character, including a space, precede it with a backslash (\). You can even type \\ to quote a backslash. For example, to list filenames that contain a question mark, type this:

```
ls *\?*
```

Single and double quotation marks quote strings of characters. They must match correctly. Single quotes are more "potent" than double quotes. Everything between double quotes is taken literally, even backslashes, with the following caveats:

✦ Wildcard characters (like * and ?) are taken literally; that is, they don't match groups of filenames.

✦ Dollar-sign variable names (described in the section "Shell Variables and the Environment," later in this part) are replaced by their values.

✦ You can quote double quotes in single quotes and vice versa.

For example, to display the text "Too #&@!;) much punctuation!" on-screen, you can use the echo command like this:

```
echo "Too #&@!;) much punctuation!"
```

If the last character on a line is a backslash, it means that the command continues on the next line.

Redirecting with Pipes and Filters

Every command has *standard input* and *standard output.* Both are normally the terminal. You can tell the shell to redirect the input or output of any command.

Redirection Character	What It Does
>	Redirects the output of a command to a file or device.
>>	Redirects the output of a command, adding it to the existing file if there is one.
<	Redirects the input of a command from a file or device.
|	Sends ("pipes") the output of one command to become the input of another command.

For example, to store a listing of files in myfiles, type this:

```
ls -l > myfiles
```

To append the listing to the end of an existing file, type this:

```
ls -l >> myfiles
```

To sort the contents of the file mydata and display the results, type this:

```
sort < mydata
```

To sort mydata and produce mysorteddata, type this:

```
sort < mydata > mysorteddata
```

You can redirect the output of one program into the input of another by using a *pipe*, which is written as a vertical bar (|). To make a file listing and send it to the printer, type this:

```
ls -l | lpr
```

You can pipe together as many programs as you want. To make a file listing, add headings with pr and print the result:

```
ls -l | pr -h "my files" | lpr
```

Programs that are usually used with redirection are called *filters*. The filters you are most likely to run into are more, sort, and maybe tee. *See* the entries for these filters in Part II.

The Shell Prompt

The shell tells you that it's ready for you to type a command by displaying a prompt string, usually a percent sign (%) for the C shell and a dollar sign ($) for the other shells. Some systems are set up with more complex prompts, including the terminal name, directory name, and so on.

Shell Variables and the Environment

Every UNIX shell has what are known as *shell variables,* which are short names for chunks of text. Several variables are set up for you, and they are called *environment variables.* You can make your own variables if you want.

The most useful environment variables are listed in the following table:

Variable	What It Contains
HOME	Pathname of your home directory (for example, `/usr/john`)
LOGNAME	Your user name (for example, `fredz`)
PATH	List of directories in which the shell looks for programs

To refer to a shell variable by name, type a dollar sign before it. Because the variable HOME automatically contains the name of your home directory, for example, type this:

```
echo $HOME
```

You see something like this:

```
/usr/elvis
```

You can use variable names within quoted text. For example, you might want to display your user name within text that includes spaces, so you need to enclose the spaces in quotes. Type this:

```
echo "My login name is $LOGNAME."
```

You see something like this:

```
My login name is elvis.
```

To see a list of all the shell variables, type **set**. To see all the environment variables, type **env** on System V or **printenv** on BSD.

Special Characters and What They Do

Nearly every punctuation character means something special to the shell. Unfortunately, the characters vary from system to system. (You can use the `stty` command to change these characters; *see* the entry for `stty` in Part II.) This section presents a roundup of the most useful special characters.

Special Character	What It Does
Enter or Return	Ends a line you're typing.
Spacebar or Tab	Separates words in commands.
Backspace, Delete, or Ctrl+H	Backspaces over errors. If none of these characters works, try # (and use stty to change it to something else, if you prefer).
;	Separates two commands on the same line.
&	After a command, tells the shell to run that command in the background and immediately return for another command. (*See* bg, fg, and kill in Part II for commands to control background programs.) A pair of ampersands (&&) is an obscure way to perform the command following the && only if the one preceding the && *succeeded.*
|	Between two commands, splices the output of the first command to the input of the second, creating a *pipeline.* (*See* the section "Redirecting with Pipes and Filters," earlier in this part.) A pair of vertical bars (||) is an obscure way to perform the command following the || only if the one preceding the || *failed.*
!	In the C shell, repeats a previously typed command, identified by what follows the !. Other than !!, which repeats the preceding command, avoid exclamation points (C shell only).
#	Whatever comment follows the # is ignored by the shell.
\	At the end of a line, indicates that the command is continued on the next line. Anywhere else, "quotoc" the following character so that it isn't treated as a special character (*see* the section "Quoting Characters on the Command Line," earlier in this part).
' or "	"Quotes" a group of characters so that they aren't treated as special characters (*see* the section "Quoting Characters on the Command Line," earlier in this part).
*	Introduces a reference to a variable (*see* "Shell Variables and the Environment," earlier in this part).
?	Wildcard that matches any single character (*see* "Wildcards," later in this part).
*	Wildcard that matches any number of characters (*see* "Wildcards," later in this part).
[ ]	Contains a group of characters to be used as wildcards (*see* "Wildcards," later in this part).
Ctrl+C	Stops programs that are stuck. If possible, use the program's exit command or the equivalent. Some programs, particularly text editors, catch Ctrl+C and wait for you to type another command. You can also try pressing the Delete key if it doesn't work as a backspace.

(continued)

Special Character	What It Does
Ctrl+D	Marks the end of input when you're typing directly to a program.
Ctrl+U or Ctrl+X	Cancels the line you're typing and starts over. If neither of these works, try @ (and use the stty command to change it to something more friendly).
Ctrl+Z	Pauses the program you're running. Use the commands fg, bg, and kill to restart or stop them. Some older shells do not support Ctrl+Z. (*See* the entries for the fg, bg, and kill commands in Part II.)

If you don't want to remember all this punctuation, just don't use special characters.

To use special characters in commands as if they were normal characters, "quote" them (*see* the section "Quoting Characters on the Command Line," earlier in this part).

+ Most shells interpret Ctrl+D as a command to log you out. So don't press it when you see the shell prompt. To terminate the program you're running, try Ctrl+C or Delete (if that's not backspace).

+ Even though your keyboard has arrow keys and the cursor moves as it should when you press them, the only programs that understand them are full-screen text editors, such as emacs and vi.

+ Do not confuse the Backspace key, which usually works everywhere, with the left-arrow key, which works only in full-screen editors.

Startup Files

System settings are stored in special files. These files contain information such as the following:

+ The type of display you are using

+ The way your keyboard functions

+ The default text editor

+ What, if any, commands are run automatically when you log in

These files are normally hidden because the filenames begin with a period. To view a list of these files, type this:

```
ls -d .*
```

You can customize these files by using a text editor. Because the commands in these files vary depending on which shell you are using and the way your system is set up, they are not described here.

You shouldn't need to change these files unless you are having a problem, such as seeing strange characters when you type. See your system administrator if you need to change your environment.

Typing Commands

Issuing a command consists of typing a series of words and then pressing the Enter (or Return) key. The first word is the name of the command, and the rest of the words are *arguments* that affect the way the command works. If the command to remove a file is rm, for example, the arguments specify which file to remove. All standard UNIX command names are lowercase, so you generally type all commands in lowercase.

Commands can be as long as you want. If you type a command that doesn't fit on a line, just keep typing, and UNIX will continue it on the next line. It may look like two lines on-screen, but until you press Enter, the computer thinks that it's one line.

Wildcards

Often, you want a command to operate on a group of files with similar names. The shell lets you use special wildcard characters to specify a group of files. This table shows the three primary kinds of wildcards:

Wildcard Character	What It Does
?	Matches any single character.
*	Matches any number of characters.
[ ]	Matches any one of the letters in the brackets.

For example, **h*** indicates all the files in the current directory that begin with an *h*; **h*g** indicates all the files that begin with *h* and end with *g*; **part[123]** indicates files named part1, part2, and part3; **part[0-9]** indicates all of part0 through part9; and ***** indicates every file in the directory.

Unlike some PC systems, UNIX wildcards do the right thing even when you use directories. For example, ***/*c** means all files that end with the letter *c* in subdirectories of the current directory.

Wildcards are handled by the shell itself, not by the command you are running. This means that all commands handle wildcards in exactly the same way. However, even when part of a command isn't a filename or if it has stars or question marks or brackets, the shell tries to make filenames out of it unless you quote it (*see* the section "Quoting Characters on the Command Line," earlier in this part).

Predicting how wildcards may work is not always easy. Before doing something dangerous with them, like deleting a bunch of files, use the `ls` command to see which filenames your wildcards match.

UNIX Commands

If it weren't for commands, UNIX wouldn't be that hard to use, really. But grep? awk? These words don't sound like commands — they sound like intestinal noises.

Because UNIX is a character-based system, though, you have to communicate with the system by typing commands. UNIX has zillions of them, and we have selected the ones that either you might want to use yourself or a UNIX guru might tell you to use.

In this part...

✓ This part lists the most useful UNIX commands. Some commands have numerous options that are rarely used, so we tell you about just the ones you are likely to run into.

✓ For each command, we include a "UNIXspeak" section, showing all the options and arguments you may have to use. In this section, information in bold is required when using the command. Text in [square brackets] is optional, so you can usually leave it out. Text in *italics* represents information that you must provide; for example, where you see *filename,* you fill in the name of the file you want to work with (don't type filename!).

alias

Creates an alias for a command or shows which aliases exist (C, BASH, and Korn shells only).

UNIXspeak (C shell)

```
alias [name ['command']]
```

UNIXspeak (Korn and BASH shells)

```
alias [name=['command']]
```

Option or Argument	Function
name	Specifies the alias name.
command	Specifies the command the name should be an alias for.

Sample

You don't want to type a long command that you use often. Instead, you want to assign it a short nickname, or *alias*. You may be tired of typing **ls -l**, for example, and would rather just type **d** to see the files in your directory.

If you use the C shell, type

```
alias d 'ls -l'
```

If you use the BASH or Korn shell, type

```
alias d='ls -l'
```

You have just created a new command, d, which is the same as ls -l.

To see which aliases you have defined, just type

```
alias
```

Aliases that you create are not saved when you log out. However, you can add this command to your startup files so that it runs automatically when you log in. *See* "Startup Files" in Part I for details.

archie

Finds files stored, or archived, on other computers. Part VII explains how to use it.

at

Schedules a command to be run at a particular time. This command is great for running time-consuming commands later, such as in the middle of the night.

UNIXspeak

`at [-f filename] [-m] time [date]`

or

`at -l`

or

`at -r job`

Option or Argument	Function
-f *filename*	Specifies the name of the file that contains the command (or commands) to run.
-m	Sends you an electronic-mail message after the command has been run.
time	Indicates when you want the command to run. Type the time in the format *hh:mm* followed by **am** or **pm**, or you can use a 24-hour clock. You can type **midnight** to run your command at night or **now** + followed by the number of minutes or hours (for example, **now + 8 hours**).
date	Indicates on which day you want the command to run. Type the date in the format month day, year, where month is the name of the month (such as **Dec** or **December**, not 12), day is the day (such as **25**), and year is the four-digit year (such as **1995**). You need the year only if the date is more than 12 months in the future.
-l	Lists the names of commands (jobs) you have already scheduled. Don't type anything on the command line after -l.
-r *job*	Cancels a command (job) you previously scheduled. Type the job number after -r. To find out the job number, use the -l option we just described.

Sample

You want to print a huge document during the night. Type

`at midnight`

After you press Enter, UNIX doesn't display a prompt. Instead, it waits for you to type the commands you want to run at midnight. Type this:

```
lpr big.report
```

Press Enter again and then press Ctrl+D when you are finished.

After you schedule a job, you can check that at hasn't forgotten about it. Type

```
at -l
```

You see a list of your scheduled jobs with their job numbers. If you decide to cancel one — for example, the job whose number is 753460300.a — type

```
at -r 753460300.a
```

Your system administrator can control who is allowed to use at. If you're not on the list, at tells you so when you try to use it.

awk

A strange programming language used by UNIX nerds to perform an amazing array of tasks.

UNIXspeak

```
awk -f program file
```

Option or Argument	Function
program	Specifies the name of the awk program to run.
file	Specifies the name of the file to modify by using the awk program or by serving as input to it.

Other versions of awk are named gawk and nawk. They all work more or less the same. *See* Chapter 9 of *MORE UNIX For Dummies* for more information about awk programming.

Sample

Programs written in awk usually read one file (the input) and create another file (the output). If you keep your checkbook in a file, for example, one check to a line, creating a program to compute the current balance is easy.

bash

Runs the Bourne Again shell.

When you use UNIX, you are always using a shell. The other shells are the Bourne shell (sh), Korn shell (ksh), and the C shell (csh). The bash command is most often useful to run a BASH script that someone has given you.

UNIXspeak

bash [script]

Sample

A friend gives you a shell script named fix.it.up that you want to run. She tells you that the script works with BASH, so you run it by typing

bash fix.it.up

bc

A handy desk calculator.

The bc calculator can do sophisticated computations, including square roots, trigonometry, conditional calculations, and converting between hexadecimal, octal, and decimal numbers. You can even define your own functions.

UNIXspeak

bc [file]

Option or Argument	Function
file	Specifies the name of a file full of bc commands. If you want to multiply just a few numbers, leave out this option.

Sample

Type **bc**. Nothing is displayed, but the calculator is now running. Type

4500 * .67

to calculate a quick discount. Whew! bc displays the answer. When you are finished doing calculations, press Ctrl+D or type **quit**.

bg

Continues a stopped job in the background. To find out which jobs are running in the background, type **jobs**.

To cancel a job that is running in the background, you use the `kill` command. To move a background job into the foreground, you use the `fg` command. (Both are described later in this part.)

Some versions of the Bourne and Korn shells don't have *job control*, which is the capability to run jobs in the background. If pressing Ctrl+Z doesn't stop a job, your shell doesn't have job control.

UNIXspeak

`bg [job]`

Option or Argument	Function
job	Specifies the job number you want to run in the background. If you don't include the job number, UNIX assumes that you mean the current job.

Sample

You start a slow program and then decide that you want to run it in the background. You press Ctrl+Z to stop the job. UNIX says something like `Stopped`. To continue the job in the background and leave the foreground free for you to give other commands, type **bg**.

cal

Prints a calendar for a month or a year.

If you type just **cal** with no month or year, you get the calendar for the current month. If you provide a year but no month, `cal` prints a 12-month calendar for the year.

To save the calendar in a text file rather than print it on-screen, redirect `cal`'s output to a file, like this:

`cal 12 1995 > christmas.trip.calendar`

Because `cal` can do calendars back to the year 1, typing **cal 95** prints a calendar for the year 95 A.D., not 1995, so watch out.

UNIXspeak

`cal [month] [year]`

Option or Argument	Function
month	Specifies the month (1 to 12) for which you want a calendar.
year	Specifies the year (1 to 9999) for which you want a calendar.

Sample

You are planning a trip for next March, but your desk calendar doesn't go that far into the future. Type

```
cal 3 1997
```

calendar

Displays appointments and reminders for today.

If you use electronic mail, you don't have to run the `calendar` program. If you have a file named `calendar` in your home directory, UNIX "automagically" runs `calendar` every day at midnight and mails you the results. When you arrive in the morning, your reminders are in your mailbox.

UNIXspeak

```
calendar
```

Sample

To use the `calendar` program, you first need a `calendar` file. Use any text editor to create a file named `calendar` in your home directory. In it, type appointments, reminders, and snide remarks, along with the date on which you want them displayed. Here is a sample `calendar` file:

```
nov 5   Send invitations for Meg's birthday party
nov 20 Bought decorations for Meg's birthday party yet?
11/30   Get Meg a present!
12/4    Meg's birthday party at 11AM!
```

When you run the `calendar` program, it displays any lines that begin with today's date. To display calendar reminders every day when you log in, add this line to the end of your `.login` or `.profile` file:

```
calendar
```

When you log in on November 30, you see this message:

```
11/30   Get Meg a present!
```

cancel

Cancels a print job (UNIX System V only).

You can skip using `lpstat` if the job you want to cancel is printing. Instead, you can specify just the name of the printer:

```
cancel lj
```

This line cancels whatever job is printing on the printer named `lj`.

UNIXspeak

```
cancel requestID
```

Option or Argument	Function
requestID	Specifies the print job you want to cancel by using the request ID number listed by the `lpstat` command (described later in this part).

Sample

To cancel the print job, you first find out its request ID by typing

```
lpstat
```

UNIX responds with a listing like this:

```
lj-1756      margyl      94832    Jan 12 10:43 on lj
lj-1762      margyl       1298    Jan 12 10:45 on lj
```

The first line describes the print job you want to cancel (you can tell because its size, 94832 characters, is big). Type

```
cancel lj-1756
```

UNIX responds

```
request "lj-1756" canceled
```

cat

Displays a file on-screen.

`cat` works only using text files. For other types of files, you have to know which program created them.

If the file you want to look at is long, use the `more` command instead, because it shows only a screen at a time.

You can also use the `cat` command (which stands for *catenate*) to combine two or more files, like this:

```
cat file1 file2 file3 > one.big.file
```

UNIXspeak

`cat` *filename*

Option or Argument	Function
filename	Specifies the name of the file you want to see.

Sample

Type

```
cat bonus.plan
```

cd

Changes the current working directory to the directory you indicate.

To move back to your home directory, type **cd**.

To move to a directory that is not a subdirectory of the current working directory, you can use a full pathname — one that begins with a slash. For example, to look around in the /usr directory (where all home directories are stored), you can type

```
cd /usr
```

If you use the BASH or Korn shell, this command moves to the last directory you were in, as shown in the following line:

```
cd -
```

UNIXspeak

`cd` [*directory*]

Option or Argument	Function
directory	Specifies the directory you want to move to. This directory becomes your current working directory. If you don't use this option, you move to your home directory.

Sample

You log in and do some work in your home directory. Next, you want to move into your budget directory to see which files are there. Type

cd budget

To move back up to the parent directory of budget, type **cd ..**

chgrp

Changes the group that has access to a file or directory (System V only).

You have to own the file or directory to use this command. To change the group ownership of a bunch of files at the same time, you can use a wildcard in the filename.

If you use BSD UNIX, you must ask your system administrator to change the group to which a file belongs.

UNIXspeak

chgrp newgroup filenames

Option or Argument	Function
newgroup	Specifies the name of the group that assumes ownership of the file (or files).
filenames	Specifies the files to change.

Sample

You just created a form to be used by your organization's accounting department. To enable the department to use it, you want to change ownership of the file from your group to the acctg group. Type

chgrp acctg snazzy.form

chmod

Changes the permissions for a file. You have to own the file or directory to use this command.

If you leave the "who" letter out of the permission, chmod assigns the permission to everyone.

Some people use numeric permission codes rather than the letter codes we favor. If someone tells you to set a file's permission to 440 or some other number, just ask for an English translation.

UNIXspeak

```
chmod [-R] permissions filenames
```

Option or Argument	Function
-R	Tells chmod to change permissions on files in subdirectories, too.
permissions	Specifies the permissions (also called the *mode*) to assign to the file (or files). Permissions consist of a letter that tells who gets the permission, a character that indicates whether to add (+) or remove (-) the permission, and a letter that tells which kind of permission.
filenames	Specifies the file (or files) to change.

Code	Who Gets the Permission
u	User who owns the file
g	Group that owns the file
o	Other (everyone else)
a	All (everybody)

Code	Which Kind of Permission
r	Read the file.
w	Write or edit the file.
x	Execute (run) the file as a program.

Sample

You create a shell script and now you want to be able to execute it. Type

```
chmod a+x newscript
```

This line allows everyone to execute the script. To prevent others from reading it, type

```
chmod go-r newscript
```

chown

Changes the owner of a file (System V only).

You have to own the file to be able to use this command. If you want to give a file to someone else, you may think that copying it to the person's home directory is enough. To give the person permission to use the file, however, it's best to change the file's ownership. After all, you can always keep a copy.

Another way to create a file with a different owner is for the new owner to copy the file. Helen can copy your report, for example. If she performs the cp command, she owns the copy. You just have to give her read permission for the file (*see* chmod).

UNIXspeak

```
chown [-R] newowner filenames
```

Option or Argument	Function
-R	Tells chown to change the ownership of files in subdirectories, too.
newowner	Specifies the name of the new owner of the file (the current owner must be you or the command doesn't work). Use the person's UNIX username.
filenames	Specifies the file (or files) to change.

Sample

You have written a report and now you want to pass it along to Helen, who will finish it up. After moving the file to Helen's home directory, type

```
chown helen final.report
```

Now Helen owns the file.

clear

Clears the screen. This command doesn't affect files or jobs — it just clears the clutter from your screen.

UNIXspeak

```
clear
```

Sample

You just tried to use the `cat` command to look at a word-processing document and your screen is full of gibberish. Type **clear**.

cmp

Compares two files and tells you the line numbers where they differ.

The problem with `cmp` is that it doesn't show you what's different about the files. For text files, you get far more information by using `diff`. On the other hand, `diff` cannot work with nontext files, and `cmp` can.

To compare three text files, *see* `diff3`.

UNIXspeak

`cmp` *onefile anotherfile*

Option or Argument	Function
onefile	Specifies the name of one of the files to compare.
anotherfile	Specifies the name of the other file to compare.

Sample

You have two versions of a letter you wrote, and you cannot tell which is the final version. Type

`cmp letter.to.dad letter.to.daddy`

If UNIX says nothing, the two letters are exactly the same, character for character. Otherwise, UNIX tells you how far it got into the file before it found something different.

compress

Shrinks a file into one "compressed" file so that it takes up less space on your disk.

When you want to get your original files back, you use `uncompress` or `zcat` (described later in this part of the book).

Compressing your files before transferring them over the network to another computer is a good idea. The smaller the file, the faster it transfers. If you want one big compressed file, create a combined file by using `ar` or `cpio` and compress the combined file.

UNIXspeak

```
compress [-v] filenames
```

Option or Argument	Function
-v	Displays how much the file (or files) shrank.
filenames	Specifies the file (or files) to compress.

Sample

You finished writing your magnum opus and mailed the manuscript to the publisher. You want to save all your manuscript files (named `chapter1`, `chapter2`, and so on) in a compressed format to save space. Type

```
compress -v chapter*
```

`compress` creates compressed files named `chapter1.Z`, `chapter2.Z`, and so on that contain freeze-dried versions of each chapter. It also deletes the original files.

See also `pack` and `unpack`.

cp

Copies one or more files.

If you know DOS, you may think that omitting the second filename tells `cp` to copy a file into the current working directory. This technique doesn't work in UNIX — instead, use a period (.) to copy a file into the current directory.

 What happens if you copy a file to a new name and a file already has that name? Assuming that you have permission to write (change) the existing file, UNIX blows it away and replaces it with the copied file. Always use the `ls` command to check that your new filename isn't already in use. And use the `-i` option to tell `cp` to ask before overwriting a file.

UNIXspeak

```
cp [-i] oldfiles newfiles
```

or

```
cp [-i] [-r] oldfiles directory[/newfiles]
```

Option or Argument	Function
-i	Ask before you replace an existing file with a copied file (only in System V Release 4).
-r	When you copy a directory, it also copies its sub-directories and creates new subdirectories as necessary.
oldfiles	Specifies the name of the file you want to copy.
newfiles	Specifies the name to give to the new copy.
directory	Specifies the name of the directory in which you want to store a copy.

Sample

You have a file that contains your January expense report. Rather than create your February expense report from scratch, you want to begin with a copy of the one for January. Type

```
cp january.expenses february.expenses
```

UNIX doesn't change the contents of january.expenses in any way — it just creates a new file called february.expenses with identical contents.

If you want to copy your finished february.expenses file into your boss's home directory, type

```
cp february.expenses /usr/harold/marqys.feb.expenses
```

By including both a path and a filename to which to copy, you tell cp to copy the file into the /usr/harold/ directory and to name the new copy margys.feb.expenses.

cpio

Creates and uncreates *cpio format* archive files. Also copies files to and from things other than hard disks. Primarily useful for copying groups of files to backup tapes and for creating an archive file to be sent over a network.

UNIXspeak

```
cpio -i [-c] [-d] [-E listname] [-u] [-v] [-V]
    [filenames]
```

or

```
cpio -o [-c] [-v] [-V]
```

or

```
[-d] [-l] -[u] [-v] [-V] directory
```

Option or Argument	Function
-c	Reads and writes archives in portable character format rather than in unportable binary format.
-d	Creates directories as needed; doesn't work with -o.
-E	Specifies that a file contains a list of filenames to be copied; doesn't work with -o or -p.
-i	Specifies that cpio extract the files from an archive back to the disk.
-l	Creates links to the files, if possible, rather than copies them; doesn't work with -i or -o.
-o	Specifies that cpio copy the files from the disk to an archive.
-p	Specifies that cpio copy the files from one directory to another on the disk.
-u	Copies files even if it means replacing existing files with the same names (watch out!); doesn't work with -o.
-v	Displays a list of filenames as it copies them.
-V	Displays a dot for each file it copies so that you can tell how fast it's going.
listname	Specifies the name of a file that contains a list of files to copy; if you use this option, don't use filenames.
filenames	Specifies the names of the files to be copied; if you use this option, don't use listname.
directory	Specifies the name of the directory to which to copy the files.

To move a bunch of files from one directory to another, including all the subdirectories, you may be able to use the cp -r command. If it doesn't work on your system, use the following magic incantation (it's ugly, but it's easier than any of the alternatives):

```
cd olddir
find * -print | cpio -pdlmv /usr/whatever/newdir
```

These commands move all the files from the olddir directory and its subdirectories to the /usr/whatever/newdir directory, creating new subdirectories as necessary. The process is rather like grafting a limb from one tree to another.

Important note: Specify the name of the new directory as a full pathname. The new directory must already exist. (Use mkdir to create the directory if necessary.) After this command runs, the files exist in both the old and new directories — use rm -r to get rid of the old directory.

The cpio command is used also for copying files to and from tapes as part of a backup procedure. *See also* tar.

Sample

You just finished a large project for which you created a bunch of files. You personally never want to see the files again, but you know that you should save them for posterity. To copy the files to an archive file, type

```
cpio -oc proj.plan report.draft report.final >
    proj.archive
```

This command creates an archive file named proj.archive that contains your project files.

Later, of course, it turns out that you have to make one or two little changes to your final report. To get the report.final file (and other files) back from the archive, type

```
cpio -icd < proj.archive
```

crontab

Makes a list of programs that you want to run on a regular schedule.

UNIXspeak

```
crontab [filename]
```

Option or Argument	Function
filename	Specifies the file that contains the list of commands and when you want to run each one.

To use crontab, you need a *crontab file:* This file contains a list of commands that you want to run and the time and day when you want to run them. A crontab file is a text file, and each line of the file contains one command, like this:

```
min   hour   DOM   month   DOW   command
```

The first five items specify when the command should be run, as described in this table:

Item	Description
min	Minute (0 to 59)
hour	Hour (0 to 23)
DOM	Day of the month (1 to 31)
month	Month (1 to 12)
DOW	Day of the week (0 to 6, where 0 is Sunday)
command	Command to run

You can use `crontab` only if your system administrator lets you. Your system administrator can also cancel commands that you have scheduled. To see your current crontab file, type

```
crontab -1
```

Sample

You want to mail yourself a message every Friday to remind yourself to pick up groceries on the way home. You create a crontab file named `my.crontab.file` (using any text editor) that contains this line:

```
0  0  *  *  5  echo "Pick up groceries!" | mail your
     user name
```

This line indicates that at midnight (0 minute and 0 hour), regardless of the day of the month (*), in all months (*), on Fridays (day 5), to send a message to yourself by way of UNIX mail. To tell the `crontab` program to run this command regularly, type

```
crontab <my.crontab.file
```

csh

Runs the C shell, optionally running a script of stored commands.

When you use UNIX, you are always using a shell. The other shells are the Bourne shell (`sh`) and the Korn shell (`ksh`). The main reason that normal people run `csh` themselves is to run a script of C shell commands that someone else wrote. But because it's nearly impossible to write a C shell script that works, most scripts are written for BASH, the Bourne shell (`sh`), or the Korn shell (`ksh`).

UNIXspeak

```
csh [scriptname]
```

Sample

Someone gives you a shell script named new.program written for the C shell. To run it, type

```
csh new.program
```

date

Tells you the current date and time, taking into account your time zone and, if appropriate, daylight saving time.

UNIXspeak

```
date
```

Far too many options let you control the exact format of the date display, but the one UNIX uses is usually clear enough. If you want to see only the date, for example, type

```
date +"%D"
```

If you want only the time, type

```
date +"%r"
```

 True weenies stay up until 2 a.m. the last weekends in April and October to be sure that daylight time changes correctly.

Sample

You wonder what time it is. Type

```
date
```

UNIX clears up any confusion you may have by displaying something like this:

```
Wed Sep 20 21:11:20 EDT
```

df

Displays how much space on your disk is free.

UNIXspeak

```
df [-b] [directory]
```

Option or Argument	Function
-b	Displays only the amount of free space in kilobytes.
directory	Displays space on the file system where that directory resides.

On System V, the directory name must be given as an absolute path starting with a slash. On BSD, any directory name will do.

The df listing includes lots of information about each *file system* to which you have access, including its total size, the amount of space that is full (used), the free space, the percentage that is full (capacity), and, if it is a *mounted directory*, on which file server it is.

Sample

You are wondering how much space is on the disk on which your home directory is stored. Assuming that your username is elvis, type

df /usr/elvis

diff

Compares two files and prints the lines in which the files differ.

UNIXspeak

diff [-b] [-i] [-w] *filename1 filename2*

or

diff [-b] [-i] [-w] *filename1 directory1*

or, for BSD UNIX only

diff [-b] [-i] [-r] [-w] *directory1 directory2*

Option or Argument	Function
-b	Treats groups of spaces (blanks) as single spaces, so it ignores spacing differences.
-i	Ignores the difference between uppercase and lowercase letters.
-r	When you're comparing two directories, specifies that subdirectories should be compared, too.
-w	Ignores all spaces and tabs.

Option or Argument	Function
filename1	Specifies one file to compare.
filename2	Specifies the other file to compare.
directory1	Specifies one directory to compare. If you tell diff to compare a file to a directory, it looks in the directory for a file of the same name and compares the two files (BSD only).
directory2	Specifies the other directory to compare. If you tell diff to compare two directories, it looks in both directories for files of the same name and compares all pairs of files with the same names. It also lists the names of files that are in one directory but not in the other.

To compare two really big files, use bdiff instead. It works just like diff, only slower. To compare files that don't contain text, use cmp. *See also* cmp, diff3, dircmp, and sdiff.

Sample

You and a friend have been collaborating on a book (a purely hypothetical example). You both have copies of the various chapters in subdirectories of your home directories. The files should be exactly the same, but are they? To compare them, type

```
diff /usr/margy/book /usr/john/book
```

UNIX looks in the two directories and compares pairs of the files with the same names. For example, it compares the following files:

```
/usr/margy/book/chapter1 and /usr/john/book/chapter1
/usr/margy/book/chapter2 and /usr/john/book/chapter2
```

Whenever UNIX finds a difference, it prints the lines from both files, like this:

```
23c23
< was the largest chocolate cake she had ever seen.
—
> was the largest chocolate bar she had ever seen.
45a
> "More vanilla!" she said again.
62d
< The End
```

The report describes the differences by telling how to turn the first file into the second. 23c23 means that line 23 in the first file (it's listed beginning with a <) should be changed to line 23 in the second file (listed beginning with a >). 45a indicates that a line should be added at the new line 45, and 62d means that line 62 of the first file should be deleted.

diff3

Compares three files.

UNIXspeak

```
diff3 filename1 filename2 filename3
```

Option or Argument	Function
filename1	Specifies one file to compare.
filename2	Specifies another file to compare.
filename3	Specifies yet another file to compare.

Sample

You and two coworkers have proofed your committee's final report. You want to compare the changes made to the three versions. Type

```
diff3 report.margy report.john. report.arnold
```

You see the differences in a format similar to that used by diff.

dircmp

Compares two directories and tells you which files are in both, which are in just one, and which are in just the other. For files in both directories, the dircmp command tells you whether the contents of the files are the same.

UNIXspeak

```
dircmp [-d] [-s] directory1 directory2
```

Option or Argument	Function
-d	For files that are in both directories, compares them by using the diff command.
-s	Doesn't say anything about files that are identical.
directory1	Specifies one directory to compare.
directory2	Specifies the other directory to compare.

The result of dircmp tells you only whether files are identical. *See also* diff, which can also compare two directories and tell you exactly how files differ.

Sample

Both you and your boss have been keeping copies of your department's monthly reports. Each of you has a directory named `Reports` that contains several files, and they seem to be more or less the same. You wonder whether either of you is missing any files and whether they all are exactly the same. Type

```
dircmp /usr/margy/Reports /usr/arnold/Reports
```

du

Tells you how much disk space your files occupy.

UNIXspeak

```
du [-a] [-s] directories
```

Option or Argument	Function
-a	Displays the space used by each file, not just by each directory.
-s	Displays the total space used for each directory, but not subdirectories.
directories	Specifies the directory or directories to include in the disk usage listing.

The size is reported in disk blocks, which are 512 characters (half a kilobyte) in UNIX System V and 1,024 (1 kilobyte) in BSD UNIX.

Sample

Your system administrator complains that your files take up too much space on the disk. "Nonsense," you reply, but then you realize that it may be better not to make her angry. Instead, you decide to refute the accusation with cold, hard evidence. Type

```
du /usr/margy
```

You see

```
162    /usr/margy/games
1492   /usr/margy/book
5403   /usr/margy/gossip
8550   /usr/margy
```

echo

Echoes whatever you type on the command line after echo and expands any wildcards by using *, ?, or [ ].

UNIXspeak

`echo [-n] stuff`

Option or Argument	Function
-n	Doesn't begin a new line after echoing the information (BSD only).
stuff	Specifies the information to echo. If it is more than one word or contains punctuation, enclose the message in quotes. The section "Quoting Characters on the Command Line," in Part I contains information about including such special characters as carriage returns, tabs, and quotation marks themselves.

Sample

You are writing a shell script and want to display a message on-screen. In the shell script, include this line:

`echo "Your report is now printing!"`

When you run the shell script, this line displays

`Your report is now printing!`

ed

Runs one of the world's ugliest line-oriented text editors. Part IV explains how to use it.

elm

Lets you read and send mail. Part V explains how to use it.

emacs

Runs a powerful screen-oriented text editor. Part IV explains how to use it.

env

Shows you information about your UNIX environment variables.

UNIXspeak

```
env
```

On some BSD systems, this command is called `printenv`. *See also* `set` and `setenv`.

Sample

You are wondering which environment variables are defined for you anyway. Type

```
env
```

You see a bunch of lines that look like this:

```
HOME=/usr/margy
TZ=AST4ADT
```

ex

A yucky, line-oriented text editor related to `ed` and `vi`. It's an extended version of `ed` (hence the name). For maximum confusion, you can also use `ex` commands within `vi`. Part IV explains how to use them all.

exit

Logs you out. When you use it in a terminal window, it closes the window.

UNIXspeak

```
exit
```

If typing **exit** doesn't work, try typing **logout**. Pressing Ctrl+D may also log you out.

When you use Motif, typing **exit** in the login window (the first window created when Motif starts up) not only closes the window but also usually logs you out.

Sample

You finish working with UNIX and want to go home. Type **exit**. You see a message saying that you have logged out.

Or you are using a terminal window in Motif, and you are finished with it. To make it go away, type **exit**. The window closes.

fg

Continues a stopped job by running it in the foreground. (Some versions of the Bourne and Korn shells cannot do this.)

UNIXspeak

fg [%job]

Option or Argument	Function
%job	Specifies the job number you want to run in the foreground. If you leave the number out, UNIX assumes that you mean the current job.

Rather than use the job number from the jobs listing, you can use the first few letters of the program that is running. If the find program is running in the background, for example, you can move it to the foreground by typing

fg %find

Sample

You are running a time-consuming program in the background by using the bg command (described earlier in this part of the book). You decide to move it to the foreground. Doing so means that you can't do any other work with your computer while the program runs, but it finishes as soon as possible.

To check that the program is still running in the background, type

jobs

You see your job listed as job number 2. Type

fg %2

Because the program runs in the foreground, you can't get any other work done, but it's running full speed.

file

Tells you whether something is a file, a directory, or something else entirely. If the thing is a file, the file command tries to guess which type of information it contains.

UNIXspeak

file *names*

Option or Argument	Function
names	Specifies the directories or files about which you want information.

The file command can determine whether a file contains ASCII text. If the file does, the file command can recognize certain types of ASCII text files, such as those that contain troff commands. It also recognizes compressed files created by using the compress or pack programs. If file cannot tell what a file contains, it suggests that the file is data. File uses some rules of thumb to guess what's in a file, so now and then it guesses wrong.

See troff, compress, and pack.

Sample

You see an object named Updates in your home directory, and you wonder whether it is a file, a directory, or something else. Type

filc Updates

You see something like this:

Update: directory

You wonder what's in the directory, so type

file Updates/*

You see a list of the filenames in the directory with a guess about each file's contents.

find

Finds one or more files, based on rules you give, and does something to them.

UNIXspeak

```
find directories [-name filename] [-user username]
    [-atime +days] [-mtime +days] [-print] [-exec
    command {} \;] [-ok command {} \;]
```

Option or Argument	Function
directories	Specifies a list of directories in which you want to begin the search. The find command searches all the subdirectories of these directories, too. If you want to start in the current directory, just type a single period (.).
-name *filename*	Specifies the name of the file (or files) you want to find. If you don't know the exact name, you can use the wildcard characters ? and *. A ? stands for any single character, and a * stands for a group of characters. You must quote the filename if you use wildcards.
-user *username*	Specifies the user who owns the files you want to find.
-atime +*days*	Specifies that you want only files that haven't been accessed (looked at) in at least *days* (the number of days). If you use a minus sign rather than a plus sign before the number of days, you get only files that were last looked at within that number of days.
-mtime +*days*	Specifies that you want only files that haven't been modified in at least *days* (the number of days). If you use a minus sign rather than a plus sign before the number of days, you get only files that were last changed within that number of days.
-print	Displays the names of files it finds. If you don't include this option, the find command may find lots of files, but it doesn't tell you about them.
-exec *command* {} \ ;	Runs *command* every time it finds a file. When it runs the command, it substitutes the name of the file it found for the {}. Be sure to type \; at the end of the command.
-ok *command* {} \ ;	Works the same way as the -exec option, except that it asks you to confirm that you want to perform the command as it finds each file.

If you want to look in several places for a file, you can type several directories on the command line, like this:

```
find . /usr/john -name chapter3 -print
```

This command looks in the current working directory (and all its subdirectories) as well as in /usr/john (and all its subdirectories) for the file chapter3.

To search for a directory, use the -type d option, like this:

```
find . -name OldVersions -type d -print
```

This command searches for a directory named OldVersions.

To search for all the files you own (assuming that your username is harold), type

```
find / -user harold -print
```

This command begins the search at the root directory (/) of the entire file system, so it may take a while.

Sample

You know that you made a file called business.plan, but you cannot find it. Perhaps it's in the wrong subdirectory. In your home directory, type

```
find . -name business.plan -print
```

UNIX tells you that a file by that name is in your Planning directory, like this:

```
./Planning/business.plan
```

Or you want to print all files with filenames that begin with *recipe*. Type

```
find -name "recipe*" -exec lpr {} \;
```

As UNIX finds each file, it runs the lpr command to print it and substitutes the filename for the {} on the command line. Notice that you must enclose the filename in quotation marks if it contains wildcard characters.

What if you are asked to delete some files because your hard drive is running out of disk space? You decide to see whether you have files that you haven't looked at in at least three months (90 days). Type

```
find -atime +90 -print
```

Alternatively, you may want to see which files you have changed within the last week. Type

```
find -mtime -7 -print
```

finger

Lists the people using your computer — with their real names, not just their UNIX usernames.

UNIX'speak

```
finger [usernames]
```

Option or Argument	Function
usernames	Specifies the user (or users) about whom you want more information.

You can also find out who is using other computers on the network. To find out who's on the xuxa system, type

```
finger @xuxa
```

The @ tells UNIX that this is the name of a system, not the name of a user. To find out more about a user on another system, type

```
finger jordan@xuxa
```

If you are on the Internet, you can get information about any user on any system on the entire network. To find out who is on an Internet system named mit.edu, for example, type

```
finger @mit.edu
```

Some Internet systems respond with general information about the system rather than a list of who's logged on, while others let you search their user directories with finger.

See also who.

Sample

You wonder who else is using your computer. Type

```
finger
```

You see a listing of usernames, real names, and other miscellaneous information. You notice a username you don't recognize, so you want more information. Type

```
finger dougm
```

You see several lines about your friend Doug Muder, including his full name, his home directory, which shell he runs, when he logged in, which project he's working on (assuming that this information is stored in a file namcd .project) in his home directory, and his plans (from a file named .plan in his home directory).

ftp

Transfers files from one computer to another over a network. Part VI explains how to use it.

gopher

Finds files stored, or archived, on other computers. Part VII explains how to use it.

grep

Finds lines in one or more files that contain a particular word or phrase.

UNIXspeak

grep [-i] [-l] [-v] *text filenames*

Option or Argument	Function
-i	Ignores case (upper- and lowercase) when you're searching.
-l	Displays only the names of the files that contain the text, not the actual lines.
-v	Specifies that you are looking for lines that *don't* contain the *text*.
text	Specifies the word or phrase to search for. If the text includes spaces or punctuation that may confuse UNIX, enclose it in quotation marks.
filenames	Specifies the file (or files) in which to search; to search all the files in the current directory, type * (asterisk).

In addition to searching for plain text, grep can search for all kinds of patterns. In fact, grep stands for *global regular expression and print*, and it searches for *regular expressions*. Luckily, regular expressions look just like text except for some punctuation that has special meaning to grep. The characters to watch out for are shown in the following table:

Character	Meaning
.	Matches any single character.
*	Matches any number of the character that precedes it. For example, .* means to match any number of any character. X* means any number of Xs.

(continued)

Character	Meaning
[ ]	Matches any one of the characters inside the brackets. For example, [ABC] matches one A, one B, or one C. [A-Z] matches any capital letter.
^	Represents the beginning of the line. For example, ^T matches a T at the beginning of a line.
$	Represents the end of the line. For example, !$ matches an exclamation point at the end of a line.
\	Tells grep to take the next character literally, not as a special character. If you want to search for I.B.M., for example, you can type I\.B\.M\.

Related programs are egrep and fgrep. egrep is more powerful but more confusing, and fgrep is faster but more limited. For your sanity's sake, stick with grep.

Sample

You are looking for the memo you wrote in which you mentioned microwaveable shelf stable foods. To search all the files in the current directory, type

```
grep "microwaveable shelf stable" *
```

You don't find the file you want. You realize that the M might be capitalized, so you tell grep to ignore capitalization by typing

```
grep -i "microwaveable shelf stable" *
```

head

Displays just the first few lines of a file (usually the first ten).

UNIXspeak

```
head [-lines] filename
```

Option or Argument	Function
-lines	Specifies the number of lines you want to see; if you omit this option, you get ten lines.
filename	Specifies the file you want to look at.

You decide that you want to see more. To see the first 20 lines, type

```
head -20 master.plan
```

To see the file one screen at a time, type

```
more master.plan
```

You can also use head to see the first few lines of the output of another command. To see just the first 15 lines of the man page about the ls command, type

```
man ls | head -15
```

On systems without a head command, you can get the same effect with the sed command. sed does all kinds of things (described later in this part of the book), but its q option displays lines at the beginning of a file. You can display the first 20 lines of the master.plan file, for example, like this:

```
sed 20q master.plan
```

Sample

You wonder what's in a file, but because it's very large, you want to see just the beginning. Type

```
head master.plan
```

You see the first ten lines of the file.

help

If your UNIX system has an online help system, this command displays possibly helpful information about commands.

UNIXspeak

```
help
```

Sample

On some UNIX systems, you can type **help**. You see a little menu of topics, and you can display information about many UNIX commands.

Most UNIX systems, however, have no help system, and you see just an error message. It's worth a try, though.

See man to learn how to use the online reference manual.

history

Lists the last 20 or so commands you typed. Works with only the C, BASH, and Korn shells.

UNIXspeak

```
history
```

TIP

If you use the C or BASH shell, you don't have to type the command again. Instead, you can re-execute the last command you gave by typing

```
!!
```

If the command you want is several commands back, you can still rerun it. To execute command number 5 in the History list, type

```
!5
```

If the command you want is the most recent command you gave that begins with *gr,* you can type

```
!gr
```

If you use the Korn shell, you can also re-execute commands. To execute the last command again, type

```
r
```

To rerun the last `grep` command, type

```
r grep
```

If you use the Bourne shell, you are out of luck.

Sample

You finally get a long, involved command to work (such as `grep` or `find`). A few minutes later, it disappears from the top of your screen (or terminal window). You want to give the command again. Type

```
history
```

You see a list of the last 20 or so commands, including the one you want to give again.

id

Tells you what your numeric user and group ID are, and, on BSD, which groups you are in.

UNIXspeak

```
id
```

Sample

You want to know your user and group IDs so that you can tell your wizard what they are when you ask for help. Type

```
id
```

UNIX responds this way:

```
uid=275(johnl), group=50(staff)
```

irc

Lets you access various Internet chat groups, which let you communicate "live" with other users connected to the Internet. Part VI explains how to use IRC.

jobs

Lists the jobs that are running in either the foreground or the background or that are stopped. (Some versions of the Bourne and Korn shells cannot do this.)

UNIXspeak

```
jobs
```

After you list your jobs, you can move jobs to the foreground or the background — *see* bg and fg.

Sample

Earlier in the day, you started a long, time-consuming job. To find out whether it is still running, type

```
jobs
```

You see a list of all the jobs you are running in either the foreground or the background, as well as any stopped jobs. (You can stop the job in the foreground by pressing Ctrl+Z.)

kill

Cancels a job that you don't want to continue.

UNIXspeak

```
kill %job
```

or

```
kill [-9] pid
```

Option or Argument	Function
job	Specifies the job you want to kill. You can use the job number listed by the j obs command or a percent sign (%) and the first few letters of the program that is running (C and Korn shells only).
-9	Tells k i l l to show no mercy in killing the program; kill it no matter what.
pid	Specifies the process ID of the job. You can use the ps command to find out the job's process ID. (*See* ps later in this part.)

If a program is truly out of control, Ctrl+Z may not stop it. In this case, you may have to find out its process ID (*pid*) to kill it. Use the ps command to see its pid (5246, for example) and then type

```
kill -9 5246
```

You can cancel only your own jobs, not jobs run by that ape in the next cubicle.

For a description of how to kill programs that do not want to die, see Chapter 16 and Chapter 23 of *UNIX For Dummies,* 2nd Edition.

Sample

You begin running a program called big.report and realize that you did something wrong. You stop the job by pressing Ctrl+Z; the message Stopped is displayed. To kill the program, type

```
kill %bi
```

Because big.report is the only program you are running that begins with the letters *bi,* it dies.

ksh

Runs the Korn shell.

When you use UNIX, you are always using a shell. The other shells are the Bourne shell (sh) and the C shell (csh). The ksh command is most often useful to run a Korn shell script that someone has given to you.

UNIXspeak

`ksh [script]`

Sample

A friend gives you a shell script named `fix.it.up` that you want to run. She tells you that the script works with the Korn shell, so you run it by typing

`ksh fix.it.up`

ln

Creates a new link to a file. Additional links can give a file more than one name or can make it live in more than one directory.

UNIXspeak

`ln ⌐-n⌐ ⌐-s⌐ existingfile newname`

or

`ln [-n] [-s] existingfiles directory`

Option or Argument	Function
-n	Tells `ln` not to clobber existing files when you're creating new links (a good idea).
-s	Tells `ln` to make a symbolic link to the file (not on older System V systems).
existingfile	Specifies the file to which you want to create a new link.
newname	Specifies the name to give to the new link.
existingfiles	Specifies the file (or files) to which you want to create a new link (or links).
directory	Specifies the directory in which you want the new link (or links).

A link to a file created by using the `ln` command works exactly the same way as the original filename for the file. You can use the `mv` command to rename the link, the `cp` command to copy the file, and the `rm` command to remove the link. (When you remove a link, the file may still remain. A file is deleted when its last link is removed.)

If you use files on other computers by way of NFS or some other system, you cannot create regular links to those files — you see a message saying `ln: different file system`. Instead, you can create *soft links* by using the `-s` option with the `ln` command.

 If a file (or a link) already has the same name as the link you are creating, some versions of `ln` destroy the exiting file (or link) and create the new one. Using the `ls` command beforehand to check whether a file already has the name you plan to use is a good idea. Then use the `-n` option of the `ln` command so that it asks before clobbering existing files.

Sample

You and your friend Katy both play backgammon, and she has a great new public domain backgammon game in the `bin` subdirectory of her home directory. Rather than make a copy of the program, which would waste space on the disk, you create a link to the file in Katy's directory. You move to your `bin` directory and type

```
ln /usr/katy/bin/backgammon backg
```

Now the filename `backg` also appears in your `bin` directory, and it refers to the same file as `/usr/katy/bin/backgammon`. If you want to create a link in the current directory by using the file's original name, you could have typed

```
ln /usr/katy/bin/backgammon .
```

If you want to create links to all the files in Katy's directory, type

```
ln /usr/katy/bin/* .
```

lp

Prints a file (in UNIX System V only).

UNIXspeak

```
lp [-c] [-d printer] [-m] [-n copies] [-o options]
   [-P pagenumbers] [-w] filename
```

Option or Argument	Function
-c	Tells `lp` to make a copy of the file to be printed; if you edit the file between the time you give the `lp` command and when it is printed, the changes don't appear in the printout.

Option or Argument	Function
-d *printer*	Specifies the printer on which you want the file printed.
-m	Tells lp to send you e-mail when the file has been printed; useful when the printer is very busy and you may have to wait your turn.
-n *copies*	Specifies the number of copies of the file to print.
-o *options*	Specifies print options, listed below.
-P *pagenumbers*	Specifies which pages to print (that's a capital *P*).
-w	Displays a message on your screen as soon as the file has printed.
filename	Specifies the file you want to print.

In response to the lp command, you see a message like this:

```
request id is lj-1024 (1 file)
```

The request ID number can be useful if you decide to cancel printing the file (*see* cancel earlier in this part of the book).

Suppose that you want to print your file on the high-quality printer in the executive suite, on a printer named execlaser. Type

```
lp -d execlaser fin.info
```

If many people share one printer, a long delay can occur before your file is printed. If you want to see a message on-screen when the file prints, you can type

```
lp -w fin.info
```

Or lp can send you electronic mail after the file has been printed, if you type

```
lp -m fin.info
```

If you want to print the output of another command, use redirection. To print a directory of files, for example, you can type

```
ls | lp
```

If you want to print several files, you can type several filenames:

```
lp fin.info memo4 letter.to.mom
```

Depending on the capabilities of your printer, you may be able to control the format of the output with the options in the following table, which you type right after the -o option:

Option	Description
nobanner	Doesn't print a banner page (a page with your username and the name of the file). UNIX usually prints a banner page before each print job to separate one from the next.
nofilebreak	Doesn't start each file on a new page.
cpi=*pitch*	Prints the file at *pitch* characters per inch. Your printer may be capable of printing at a limited number of pitches, usually only 10 or 12.
lpi=*lines*	Prints the file at *lines* lines per inch (usually six). Some printers can print eight lines per inch.
length=*inches*i	Prints pages that are *inches* inches long (be sure to include the small *i* at the end of the option).
length=*lines*l	Prints pages that are *lines* lines long (be sure to include the small *l*).
width=*chars*	Prints a maximum of *chars* characters per line.
width=*inches*i	Prints pages that are a maximum of *inches* inches wide.

To print several files with no page breaks between them, for example, you can type

```
lp -o nofilebreak fin*
```

Sample

You create a text file that contains some important financial information that you want to pass along to your boss. Type

```
lp fin.info
```

After you print it, you decide that you want two more copies, so type

```
lp -n 2 fin.info
```

lpq

Lists the status of available printers (in BSD UNIX only).

UNIXspeak

```
lpq [-a] [printer]
```

Option or Argument	Function
-a	Lists information about all printers.
printer	Specifies the printer you want to know about; if you don't specify the printer, it assumes a default, usually the printer closest to you.

Sample

You have tried to print several large documents, but they have yet to appear on the printer. To look at the print queue for your printer, which is named *laser*, type

```
lpq laser
```

UNIX responds

```
no entries
```

If no entries are displayed, maybe the documents are waiting to print on another printer. To see the print queues for all the available printers, type

```
lpq -a
```

lpr

Prints a file (in BSD UNIX only).

UNIXspeak

lpr [-P*printer*] *filename*

Option or Argument	Function
-P *printer*	Specifies which printer to use.
filename	Specifies the file you want to print.

You can also print the output of another command. For example, this line shows how to print a man page:

```
man chmod | lpr
```

Sample

To print a file named status_report, type

```
lpr status_report
```

56

If you decide to print it on a printer named `hplj`, type

```
lpr -Phplj status_report
```

lpstat

Lists the status of available printers (in UNIX System V only).

UNIXspeak

```
lpstat [-a all] [-d] [-p printers]
```

Option or Argument	Function
-a all	Lists all printers that are available.
-d	Lists your default printer (the printer on which your files print unless you specify otherwise).
-p *printers*	Displays the status of the printer (or printers) you name.

To find all the printers on the network, type

```
lpstat -a all
```

You see a list of printers, one per line, with the name and status of each one. If the printer is `accepting requests`, you can use it. To find out whether several print jobs are in the print queue for a particular printer — one named `execlaser`, for example — type

```
lpstat -p execlaser
```

Sample

You send a large document to the printer, but you change your mind. To find out its request ID, type

```
lpstat
```

You see a list of the print jobs waiting to be printed on your printer, including the request ID of each one. To cancel the job with request ID `hplj-78344`, type

```
cancel hplj-78344
```

ls

Lists the files in a directory.

UNIXspeak

```
ls [-a] [-l] [-p] [-r] [-R] [-t] [-x] [pathname]
```

Option or Argument	Function
-a	Displays all the files and subdirectories, including hidden files (with names that begin with a dot).
-l	Displays detailed information about each file and directory, including permissions, owners, size, and when the file was last modified.
-p	Displays a slash (/) at the end of each directory name to distinguish them from filenames.
-r	Displays files in reverse order.
-R	Includes the contents of all subdirectories, too.
-t	Displays files in order of modification time.
-x	Displays the filenames in columns across the screen.
pathname	Names the file or directory to list.

If you want to see the sizes and modification dates of all your files, you can type

```
ls -al
```

You can combine several options together after one dash, to save typing. This "long format" listing looks like this:

```
-rwxr-xr-x  2  mgmt john   14675 Nov 9   15:34
    fin.info
-rw-rw-rw  1  mgmt margy   3827 Nov 6   19:43
    baked.beans
drw-rw-rw- 16  mgmt margy    128 Oct 1   11:31   Mail
```

This listing contains the following eight columns:

Column	Description
Permissions	The first letter indicates whether it is a file (-) or a directory (d). The remaining nine characters are in groups of three: The first group shows the owner's permissions, the second group shows the group's permissions, and the third group shows everyone else's permissions. Each group of three characters includes the read (r or -), write (w or -), and execute (x or -) permission. A dash indicates that the permission isn't granted. The permissions -rwxr-xr—, for example, indicate that it is a file (not a directory); its owner can read, write, and execute it; its group can read or execute it but not write on it; and everyone else can read it but not write or execute it.

(continued)

Column	Description
Links	The number of names (links) that the file has. For directories, this sum is the number of files in the directory plus 2.
Group owner	The name of the group that owns this file.
User owner	The name of the user who owns this file.
Size	The size of the file in bytes (characters).
Mod. date	The date on which the file was last modified.
Mod. time	The time when the file was last modified.
Filename	The name of the file.

Suppose that the directory listing shows that you have a subdirectory named `bin` (the `bin` directory usually contains programs you use). To see what it contains, type

```
ls -l bin
```

Suppose that you are looking for a filename that begins with `bud`. You hope that it is in your home directory or a subdirectory of it. Type

```
ls -R bud*
```

To list all the information about your files, sorted in reverse order of modification time, type

```
ls -ltr
```

If a directory listing is too long to fit on-screen, redirect its output to the `more` command so that you can see one page at a time, like this:

```
ls -al q* | more
```

Alternatively, you can list the filenames across the screen by typing this line:

```
ls -x
```

Sample

You are working in your home directory and want to see a list of the files in it. Type

```
ls
```

But what about your hidden files, such as `.login` and `.profile`? To see information about all your files, type

```
ls -a
```

lynx

A text-based program used to find and display information from the World Wide Web (WWW). Part VII explains how to use it.

mail

Lets you read and send mail. Part V explains how to use it.

man

Displays the reference manual page about a UNIX command.

UNIXspeak

```
man [-] [-k keywords] topic
```

Option or Argument	Function
-	If your system usually presents manual pages one screen at a time, this option displays them without stopping, which is useful in redirecting the output of man to a file or to the printer.
-k keywords	Specifies one or more keywords to search for. You see all man pages that contain the keyword (or keywords) in their header lines.
topic	Specifies the topic you want information about. The man pages are usually descriptions of UNIX commands, with a small number of general topics.

To print a manual page, you can type

```
man ls | lp
```

If you use BSD UNIX, redirect output to lpr instead.

If you use Motif or another X Windows system, try running xman rather than man.

Sample

You forgot the options that you can use with the ls command, so type

```
man ls
```

On some systems, the manual pages scroll right off the top of your screen (other systems automatically use more with man so that you see one screen at a time). Type

```
man ls | more
```

To save this information for later perusal or inclusion in a user's manual you are writing for your department, type

```
man ls > ls.info
```

mesg

Lets you control whether other people can use the write command to interrupt you with on-screen messages.

UNIXspeak

```
mesg [n|y]
```

Option or Argument	Function
n	Prevents messages from other users from popping up on your screen.
y	Allows messages to appear on your screen.

Using electronic mail is preferable to using write when you want to communicate with other users.

Sample

Another user is sending messages to you. The messages distract you and mess up your screen. Type

```
mesg n
```

Now, when users try to send messages, they see

```
Permission denied.
```

mkdir

Creates a new directory.

UNIXspeak

```
mkdir directory
```

Option or Argument	Function
directory	Specifies the name of the new directory. If the name doesn't begin with a slash, the new directory is created as a subdirectory of the current working directory. If the name begins with a slash, the name defines the path from the root directory to the new directory.

You must have permission to write in a directory to create a subdirectory in it. For the most part, you should create directories in your own home directories or subdirectories of it.

Sample

You want a place to store some files temporarily. In your home directory, type

```
mkdir Temp
```

The next time you use the ls command, the Temp directory appears in your home directory.

more

Displays information one screen at a time so that you can read it easily.

UNIXspeak

```
more [ l ] [ r] [-s] [-u] [+linenum] [+/text] [filename]
```

Option or Argument	Function
-l	Ignores form feed characters in the file (Ctrl+L, which starts a new page). Use this option if the file has a great deal of tiny pages of text.
-r	Displays control characters instead of performing their function. For example, the control character Ctrl+H is a backspace: Rather than backspace, this option displays Ctrl+H as ^H.
-s	Squeezes out extra blank lines by displaying only one blank line.
-u	Ignores underscore and backspace characters, which can otherwise make text unreadable on-screen.
+linenum	Displays the file (or whatever the input to more is) as line linenum.
+/text	Begins displaying text two lines before the first time text appears.
filename	Specifies the file to display.

When more pauses at the end of a screen, you can press any of the following keys:

Key	Meaning
Spacebar	Displays the next screen of text.
Enter or Return	Displays the next line of text.
h	Displays help about what these keys mean.
q	Quits displaying this file.
/	Searches for some text. Type the text to search for immediately after the /, followed by Enter or Return.

The more command is frequently used with redirection to display the output of another command. To see a long directory listing one screen at a time, for example, type

```
ls | more
```

Sample

You receive a long memo in a text file. To display it on your screen, type

```
more long.memo
```

After displaying one screen of text, more pauses. Press the spacebar to see the next screen of text.

mv

Renames a file or moves it from one directory to another.

UNIXspeak

```
mv [-i] oldname newname
```

or

```
mv [-i] filename directory[/newname]
```

Option or Argument	Function
-i	Tells mv to prompt you before it replaces an existing file with a moved or renamed file (works only in UNIX System V Release 4).
oldname	Specifies the existing file you want to rename.
newname	Specifies the new name to use for the file.

Option or Argument	Function
filename	Specifies the file you want to move.
directory	Specifies the directory to which you want to move the file.

You can move and rename a file at the same time. For example, if you want to move your new.recipe file into your Recipes directory and rename it at the same time, you can type

    mv new.recipe Recipes/veg.lasagne

You can also rename and move entire directories. Suppose that you want to rename your Recipes directory. Type

    mv Recipes Food

The directory gets a new name. This operation doesn't affect the files in the directory.

Or suppose that you want to move your Recipes directory to be a subdirectory of your Personal directory. Type

    mv Recipes Personal

If another file already has the name you want to use, mv deletes it without telling you and replaces it with the renamed or moved file. To avoid this situation, use the -i option (for UNIX System V Release 4 users only). Or use the ls command first to make sure that no file in the directory has the name you want to use.

Sample

A coworker gives you a file named old.budget. You want to give it a better name, so type

    mv old.budget 1993.budget

Then you decide to move it into your Budget directory. Type

    mv 1993.budget Budget

nice

Runs a command with lower priority so that it doesn't hog the computer.

UNIXspeak

    nice command [arguments] [&]

Option or Argument	Function
command	Specifies the command you want to run.
arguments	If you want to provide arguments for the command, type them just as you would if you weren't using the nice command.
&	Runs the command in the background; no one ever uses nice to run programs in the foreground.

Many shells automatically nice anything that is begun with &, so you may not have to.

Sample

You usually run your monthly invoice report by typing

```
invoice.rpt 1994.12
```

except that you use different filenames for the argument. 1994.12 contains the data for one month.

The program slows the computer down, however, so you decide to run it in the background with low priority so that it takes longer but doesn't slow the system down so much. Type

```
nice invoice.rpt 1994.12 &
```

You see the process ID (pid) of the job and another prompt, so you can work in the foreground as the program runs in the background.

nn

Lets you read messages posted to Usenet newsgroups. Part VIII explains how to use it.

pack

Shrinks a file into one "packed," or compressed, file so that it takes up less space on your disk.

UNIXspeak

```
pack filenames
```

Option or Argument	Function
filenames	Specifies the files to compress.

When you want to get your files back from a packed file, use unpack (described later in this part of the book).

See also compress and uncompress. The compress command usually does a better job than pack does.

Sample

You finish writing a large report and want to save it in a compressed format to save space. Type

```
pack long.report
```

pack makes a packed file named long.report.z that contains a shrunken version of the file and deletes the original file.

passwd

Changes your password.

UNIXspeak

```
passwd [-s]
```

Option or Argument	Function
-s	Displays status information, including your username, whether you have a password, and when you last changed it. This option does *not* display your password, though. (If you forget your password, your administrator can change it to something else.)

You have to know your password to be able to change it. If you forget your password, ask your system administrator to give you a new one. Many versions of passwd try to enforce such rules as the password must be at least seven characters, contain digits, and otherwise be hard to remember. Often, if you try an unacceptable password three or four times, passwd gives up and accepts it.

Sample

Type

```
passwd
```

UNIX prompts you for your current password to prove that you really are you. Then it asks you to enter a new password twice. Because the password doesn't appear on-screen, typing it twice ensures that no typo occured when you typed it the first time.

pico

Runs an easy-to-use, screen-oriented text editor. Part IV explains how to use it.

pine

Lets you read and send mail. Part V explains how to use it.

pr

Formats a text file with page numbers, line numbers, or other options so that the file looks nice when you print it.

UNIXspeak

```
pr [-a] [-d] [-f] [-F] [-h text] [-l lines] [-m] [-n]
   [-o offset] [-t] [-w width] [+pagenum] [-columns]
   filenames
```

Option or Argument	Function
-a	Prints lines across the page. This option is great when you have lots of short lines.
-d	Double-spaces the output.
-f	Uses form feed characters rather than blank lines to move to the top of a new page.
-F	Wraps long lines to the beginning of the next line rather than cut them off. (Stands for *fold*.)
-h *text*	Prints *text* as the header at the top of each page. If you omit this option, pr prints a header that consists of the filename and the date the file was last changed.
-l *lines*	Sets the page length to *lines* lines. If you omit this option, the page length is 66 lines, which is correct when you're printing at six lines per inch on 11-inch paper.
-m	Merges several files together and prints each one in a separate column.
-n	Numbers the lines of the file.
-o *offset*	Prints *offset* extra spaces at the beginning of each line to make a wider left margin. This option is useful if you plan to punch holes in the paper or bind it.
-t	Suppresses printing of page headers or blank lines at the end of a file.

Option or Argument	Function
-w width	Sets the line width to width characters. If you leave this option out, the line width is 72 characters. This option is useful if you have a file with multiple columns.
+pagenum	Begins printing at page pagenum.
-columns	Prints the file in multiple columns, as in a newspaper. Columns is the desired number of columns.
filenames	Specifies the file (or files) you want to format for printing.

To put line numbers at the beginning of each line, type

```
pr -n -h choco.story | lp
```

Later, after you modify the file, you want to print the original and new version side by side. Also, you want to add a one-inch (ten-character) left margin. Type

```
pr -o10 -m choco.story choco.story.new | lp
```

 You can use pr only with text files, not with word-processing documents, PostScript output files, or other data files.

Sample

To format a file named choco.story, type

```
pr choco.story | lp
```

This command formats the choco.story file and redirects the result to the lp command for printing. (If you use BSD UNIX, use the lpr command rather than lp.)

The last (fourth) page is smudged, so you reprint it by typing

```
pr +4 choco.story | lp
```

ps

Displays information about your processes (jobs).

UNIXspeak (BSD UNIX)

```
ps [-a] [-l] [-ttty] [-u] [-x]
```

Option or Argument	Function
-a	Displays information about all processes; if you omit this option, you see only your processes.
-l	Displays a longer, more detailed version.
-t*tty*	Displays a list of processes that were started by terminal *tty.*
-u	Displays a "user-oriented" report with additional information.
-x	Displays all processes that are running in the background and not using a terminal.

UNIXspeak (UNIX System V)

ps [-a] [-e] [-f] [-t *ttys*] [-u *usernames*]

Option or Argument	Function
-a	Includes information about almost all processes, not just processes you started.
-e	Displays all the processes in the entire system.
-f	Displays a "full," more detailed listing.
-t*ttys*	Displays a list of processes that were started by terminal (or terminals) *ttys.*
-u*usernames*	Displays a list of processes that were started by the specified username(s).

The ps command produces a listing with one process per line. The columns you see depend on whether you use BSD UNIX or UNIX System V and which options you use.

Column	Description
PID	Process ID, the unique number assigned to the process. You use the PID to kill the process if it gets out of control (**see** kill, earlier in this part of the book).
TTY or TT	Terminal ID where the process was run.
TIME	The number of minutes and seconds the process has run, counting only the time during which the process had the computer's full attention.
COMMAND	Command that began the process, more or less.
UID or USER	Username of the user who began the process.
PPID	PID of the process's *parent process* (the process that started this process). Sometimes, typing one command starts several processes.

Column	Description
C	Magic number related to how much CPU time the program has used lately.
STIME	Start time (the time of day when the process began). If the process began more than 24 hours ago, this column shows the date.
STAT	Status of the process (R or 0 means that it is running right now).
%CPU	Percentage of the available central processing time the process has taken recently
%MEM	Percentage of the available system memory the process has taken recently.
SZ	Total memory size of the program, measured in kilobytes.
RSS	How much memory the process is using right now, measured in kilobytes.

To find out how long you have been logged in, the number of people using your computer, and other fun facts, try typing **uptime**. You can also use the w command for information about users and processes.

Sample (BSD UNIX)

You wonder whether the process you ran in the background is still running. Type

```
ps
```

to see a list of all your processes. To see more information about them, type

```
ps -l
```

No option lets you see processes started by one particular user. Instead, you can use grep to find them. To see all the processes that were started by lee, type

```
ps -aux | grep lee
```

Sample (UNIX System V)

You think that a program may be running amok, so type

```
ps
```

to see a list of all your processes. To see more information about them, type

```
ps -f
```

You want to check on your friend Lee's processes too, so type

ps -u lee

pwd

Displays the name of the current working directory.

UNIXspeak

pwd

Sample

You are lost and want to know which directory you are in (what the current working directory is). So type

pwd

You see a pathname like this:

/usr/margy/Recipes

rcp

Copies files to or from another computer (rcp stands for *remote copy*). Part VI explains how to use it.

red

Runs a restricted (dumb) version of the line-oriented text editor, ed. You can edit the files in only the current directory, and you cannot give shell commands. Even less useful than ed.

rehash

Updates the table of UNIX commands and the programs they run (used only with the C shell).

UNIXspeak

rehash

If you don't run rehash, UNIX can find your new program only when it is in the current directory. After you run rehash, it can find the program no matter what the current directory is. The program must be stored in a directory that is included in your PATH environment variable.

Sample

You have just written a shell script, which is stored in a file named do.it in your bin directory. To enable UNIX to find this new program when you type **do.it,** you update UNIX's command table by typing

```
rehash
```

rlogin

Logs in to another computer (rlogin stands for *remote login*). **See** Part VI, which explains how to use it.

rm

Deletes (removes) a file permanently.

UNIXspeak

rm [-i] [-r] *filenames*

Option or Argument	Function
-i	Asks you to confirm that you want to delete each file.
-r	Deletes an entire directory and the files it contains. Watch out — you can do a great deal of damage with this option! Always use the -i option.
filenames	Specifies the file (or files) to delete.

If other links (names) to the file exist, the file continues to exist. rm just deletes the name (link) you specify. A file actually dies when its last link (name) is deleted.

If you delete a file by mistake, talk to your system administrator immediately. If you're lucky, a backup copy of the file may be on tape.

Sample

You made a test file and now you are finished with it. Type

```
rm text.junk
```

The file disappears from your directory.

Suppose that you want to delete all your old budget files. First, you make sure that you know what you are planning to delete. Type

```
ls budget.93.*
```

If the list of files you see looks right, then delete them:

```
rm budget.93.*
```

rmdir

Deletes (removes) a directory.

UNIXspeak

```
rmdir directory
```

Option or Argument	Function
directory	Specifies the directory you want to delete (the directory must be empty already).

To delete a directory and all the files in it, you can use the rm -ir command (*see* rm earlier in this part of the book). You cannot delete the current working directory, so move to its parent (by typing **cd ..**) before deleting a directory.

Sample

After making backup copies of your files on a tape, you want to delete your Budget directory. First, you need to make sure that it doesn't contain anything you want to keep, so type

```
ls Budget
```

All the files listed are files you want to delete, so type

```
rm Budget/*
```

The Budget directory is now empty, so type

```
rmdir Budget
```

rn

Lets you read messages posted to Usenet newsgroups. Part VIII explains how to use it.

rsh

Runs a command on another computer (rsh stands for *remote sh*ell).
Part VI explains how to use it.

script

Saves the conversation you are having with UNIX in a text file (stores
everything you type and everything UNIX types back at you). Works
with BSD UNIX and UNIX System V Release 4 only.

UNIXspeak

```
script [-a filename]
```

Option or Argument	Function
-a *filename*	Specifies the file in which to store the information (if the file exists, it adds the new information to the end). If you don't use this option, script stores the text in a file named typescript.

If you are having trouble using the system, this command can be a
useful way to document your input and the system's responses.

Sample

You want to record your commands and UNIX's responses so that
you can show your new trainee how to do something. Before giving
the first command, type

```
script
```

Then you give your usual series of commands. After you finish, type
exit to leave script.

sdiff

Compares two files by listing them side by side.

UNIXspeak

```
sdiff [-s] [-w width] filename1 filename2
```

Option or Argument	Function
-s	Suppresses printing of identical lines and prints only those that differ.
-w *width*	Specifies the width of your screen (use -w 80).
filename1	Specifies one file to compare.
filename2	Specifies the other file to compare.

If the lines in the two files differ, UNIX puts a symbol in the column between the two files. If the line is in only the first file, the symbol is <; if it exists in only the second file, the symbol is >; and if the lines are different in the two files, the symbol is |.

See also cmp, diff, and diff3.

Sample

Your boss makes some edits to your file. You want to know what they are, so you compare the edited version to your original by typing

```
sdiff memo4 memo4.original
```

sed

Lets you use prerecorded commands to make changes to text (sed stands for *stream editor*).

UNIXspeak

```
sed [-f commandfile] [commands] filenames
```

Option or Argument	Function
-f *commandfile*	Specifies the file that contains the sed commands.
commands	Specifies sed commands to perform. If they contain spaces or punctuation, enclose the commands in quotes.
filenames	Specifies the file(s) that contains the original text.

Sample

You want to look at the first 20 lines of a file. The q command quits when it gets to the specified line, so type

```
sed 20q longfile
```

`sed` displays the file and quits after the 20th line. Or you can display the first 15 lines of output from the manual page about the `ls` command, like this:

```
man ls | sed 15q
```

Or you want to replace all instances of Abel with Baker in a text file. You can use the `s` command, like this:

```
sed "s/Abel/Baker/g" letter3 > letter3.new
```

This command reads the file `letter3`, changes Abel to Baker wherever it occurs, and stores the result in `letter3.new`.

See Chapter 8 in *MORE UNIX For Dummies* for more info on writing `sed` commands. The commands for `sed` are almost exactly the same as the ones for `ed`, described in Part IV.

set

Sets a shell variable to the value you specify or displays the value of the shell variable.

UNIXspeak (Bourne, BASH, and Korn shells)

```
set
```

UNIXspeak (C shell)

```
set [variable = value]
```

Option or Argument	Function
variable	Specifies the variable whose value you want to set.
value	Specifies the value you want to assign to the variable.

UNIXspeak (any shell)

To see a list of the defined variables in your shell, type

```
set
```

To see the value of one variable, use the `echo` command like this:

```
echo $WORKDIR
```

UNIX forgets the variables you define when you log out. If you want to define a variable so that UNIX remembers it, add it to your `.login` or `.profile` file.

To get rid of a variable right away rather than wait until the next time you log out, use the `unset` command.

Sample (Bourne, BASH, and Korn shells)

You want to set a shell variable to the name of a directory you frequently use. Type the following line (no spaces allowed):

```
WORKDIR=/usr/fred/project/
```

Now you can use `WORKDIR` as the project directory name in your commands, like this:

```
cd $WORKDIR
```

In the Bourne and Korn shells, variable names are usually spelled with capital letters.

Sample (C shell)

You want to set a shell variable to the name of a directory you frequently use. Type

```
set workdir=/usr/fred/project/
```

Now you can use `workdir` as the project directory name in your commands, like this:

```
cd $workdir
```

In the C shell, variable names are usually spelled with small letters.

To set the value of an environment variable (a variable that is maintained by the shell and contains information about the shell environment) in the C shell, you use the `setenv` command, described later in this part of the book. In the Bourne and Korn shells, type `export WORKDIR` to make `WORKDIR` an environment variable.

setenv

Sets the value of an environment variable (C shell only).

UNIXspeak

```
setenv [variable [value]]
```

Option or Argument	Function
variable	Specifies the variable whose value you want to set.
value	Specifies the value you want to assign to the variable. If you leave it out, UNIX assigns nothing to the variable (the "null" value).

To see a list of your environment variables and their values, type

```
setenv
```

Notice that there is no equal sign in the setenv command, even though you have to use one with the set command.

Sample

The PATH variable contains the list of directory pathnames that UNIX searches whenever you type the name of a program. Frequently run programs should be stored in directories on the PATH list.

Suppose that you want to see your PATH list. Type

```
echo $PATH
```

Suppose that you have a bin subdirectory of your home directory and that it contains programs. You want to add this directory to your PATH list. Type

```
setenv PATH $PATH:/usr/margy/bin
```

This line sets the PATH variable to its current value, followed by the pathname /usr/margy/bin (substitute your username in place of margy).

sh

Runs the Bourne shell.

UNIXspeak

```
sh [scriptname]
```

Option or Argument	Function
scriptname	Name of a file that contains a Bourne shell script.

When you use UNIX, you are always using a shell. The other shells are the C shell (csh), BASH, and the Korn shell (ksh). You're likely to run sh yourself only to run a shell script that someone has given you.

TIP

If you receive a *shar message* by way of electronic mail, you run it as a shell script to create a file. A shar message is a sneaky way to send nontext files (short programs and shell scripts) through the mail. To recover the file from a shar message, save the message as a text file, use a text editor to remove all the lines from the beginning of the file to the first line that begins with a #, and then feed the file to the shell. If you save the shar message in a file called `shar.msg`, for example, you type

```
sh shar.msg
```

This command runs the script in the shar file and creates the program files it contains. (At the beginning of most shar messages is a list of the files that the shar message creates.)

Sample

A friend gives you a shell script named `check.all.files` that you want to run. She tells you that the script works with the Bourne shell, so you run it by typing

```
sh check.all.files
```

sleep

Makes UNIX wait a little while, which is measured in seconds.

UNIXspeak

```
sleep time
```

Option or Argument	Function
time	Specifies the number of seconds to wait.

You won't find much reason to use this command except in a shell script. If you want to execute a command at a particular time, *see* at and `crontab`.

Sample

In a shell script, you want to pause before performing a command. You include this line in the shell script:

```
sleep 5
```

When you run the script, it pauses for five seconds when it executes the `sleep` command.

sort

Sorts the lines in a text file.

UNIXspeak

```
sort [-b] [-d] [-f] [-i] [-m] [-M] [ n] [ r] [ u]
    [+fields] filename [-o outputfile]
```

Option or Argument	Function
-b	Ignores spaces at the beginning of the line.
-d	Uses dictionary sort order and ignores punctuation.
-f	Ignores capitalization while sorting.
-i	Ignores nonprinting control characters.
-m	Merges two or more input files into one sorted file.
-M	Treats the first three characters of each line as a three-letter month abbreviation and sorts by month order (Jan before Feb and so on).
-n	Sorts based on the number at the beginning of the line. With this option, 99 precedes 100 rather than follows it, as it does in usual alphabetical order.
-r	Sorts in reverse order. You can combine this option with any other option.
-u	If the same line occurs in the file more than once, outputs it only once (stands for *unique*).
+*fields*	Considers each line to contain a series of fields (fields are separated by tab characters). When you're sorting, *fields* specifies the number of fields to skip from the left end of the line. For example, `sort +2` sorts beginning at the third field on each line.
filename	Specifies the file that contains the text to be sorted.
-o *outputfile*	Specifies that `sort` should send the sorted output to a file and specifies the name of the file.

You can also sort the output of another command. For example, you can sort the list of lines that `grep` outputs, like this:

```
grep "eggplant parm" recipe.list | sort
```

The output of a number of commands (including ls) consists of fields separated by tabs, so you can sort it by using the +fields option. To sort a listing of files in numeric order by the fifth field (the file size), for example, you can type

```
ls -l | sort -n +5
```

Sample

You want to sort a list of names into alphabetical order. Type

```
sort name.list > sorted.list
```

The sorted text is stored in a new file named sorted.list.

spell

Looks through a text file and reports which words are not in the UNIX dictionary.

UNIXspeak

```
spell [-b] [+wordlist] filenames
```

Option or Argument	Function
-b	Uses British spellings.
+wordlist	Adds the contents of the file named wordlist to the UNIX dictionary so that words contained in the wordlist file are not considered to be misspelled.
filenames	Specifies the file (or files) to be spell-checked.

spell works only with text files. If you use a word processor, use its built-in spell-checker instead. Also try running ipspell, an interactive spell-checker that may be on your system.

Sample

You use a text editor to write a memo, and you want to check your spelling. Type

```
spell memo.to.bob
```

Several words are rejected as misspelled. Then you remember that your friend Harold maintains a "jargon file" of nonstandard words you frequently use. Type

```
spell +/usr/harold/jargon memo.to.bob
```

Fewer words are seen as misspelled.

stty

Sets the options for your terminal.

UNIXspeak

`stty [charname char] [sane] [[-]tostop] [-a]`

Option or Argument	Function
charname	Specifies the terminal control character you want to see. Refer to the following table to see what these characters are.
char	Specifies the key (or keys) you want to use for this terminal control character.
sane	Returns your terminal to a "sane" state, which is useful if an editor dies and leaves your terminal in a state in which characters don't echo.
-tostop	Turns off terminal stop mode so that output from background jobs can be displayed on your screen.
tostop	Turns on terminal stop mode to prevent output from background jobs from being displayed on your screen. (Terminal stop mode is usually on, unless you have turned it off.)
-a	Displays all the terminal settings.

You can change dozens of terminal settings, but you should leave most of them alone. The following table shows terminal control characters you may want to set.

Name	Typical Character	Meaning
erase	Ctrl+H	Erases (backspaces over) the preceding character.
kill	Ctrl+U	Discards the line typed so far.
eof	Ctrl+D	Marks the end of input to a program.
swtch	Ctrl+Z	Pauses the current program.
intr	Ctrl+C	Interrupts or kills the current program.
quit	Ctrl+\	Kills the current program and writes a core file.

To set your terminal options every time you log in, include your `stty` commands in your `.profile` or `.login` file.

Sample

You want to use Ctrl+Q as the Backspace key on your terminal because you used it on your previous system. Type

```
stty erase '^q'
```

Be sure to put quotes around the key name so that `stty` and the shell don't get confused. The caret (^) means that you press the Ctrl key along with the letter, so `'^q'` means Ctrl+Q. Type the Delete or Rubout key as `'^?'`.

To list all your terminal settings, type

```
stty
```

tail

Displays the last few lines of a file.

UNIXspeak

```
tail [-r] [-lines] filename
```

Option or Argument	Function
-r	Displays the lines in reverse order.
-lines	Specifies the number of lines you want to see (counting from the end of the file).
filename	Specifies the file you want to see the end of.

Suppose you maintain a log file of changes to an important database. You want to see the last 20 changes in reverse chronological order, so type

```
tail -r -20 log.file
```

You can also use `tail` to see the last lines of output from another command. If you want to see the last ten changes Tonia made to the log file, for example, you can type

```
grep "Tonia" log.file | tail
```

Sample

You wonder whether you remembered to include a P.S. at the end of a memo you wrote. Type

```
tail memo.to.frank
```

You see the last ten lines of the file.

talk

Lets you talk to another computer user by typing messages to each other on-screen.

UNIXspeak

```
talk user[@computer]
```

Option or Argument	Function
user	Specifies the username of the person with whom you want to chat.
computer	Specifies the name of the computer on which the person is logged.

To talk to someone else on the network, use the person's e-mail address as the computer name. If someone wants to talk to you but you don't want to talk back, you don't have to. To prevent people from talking to you at all, type **mesg n**.

Sample

You use the `finger` command to determine that your friend Deb is logged on to the computer system in another building on your campus. According to `finger`, she is using a computer called `samba`. To chat with her, type

```
talk deb@samba
```

Deb sees a message on her screen like this:

```
Message from Talk_Daemon@iecc at 2:32 ...
talk: connection requested by margy@iecc
talk: respond with: talk margy@iecc
```

Deb wants to talk with you, so she types

```
talk margy@iecc
```

Now the top part of the screen shows what you type, and the bottom part shows what Deb types. (Deb sees the same thing, but vice versa.) Type messages to each other. After you finish, sign off by pressing Ctrl+D.

tar

Copies a file to or from an archive file, backup tape, or floppy disk.

UNIXspeak

```
tar c|r|t|u|x[l][o][v][w][0-9][f tarfile] filenames
```

Option or Argument	Function
c	Copies files to a new archive file or tape.
r	Copies files to the end of an existing tape.
t	Displays a list of all the files stored on the tape.
u	Copies files to the tape unless they are already there. If a previous version of a file is on the tape, it copies the new version to the tape (tape only).
x	Copies (extracts) files *from* the archive file or tape.
l	Displays error messages if it cannot find files.
o	When you're extracting files (copying them from the archive file or tape), changes the ownership of the files to you rather than to their original owners.
v	Displays the names of the files as it copies them, plus a (for archive when you're copying to an archive file or tape) or x (for extract when you're copying from an archive file or tape).
w	Asks you to confirm the copying of each file.
0-9	A single digit says which unit to use. If you have only one tape or floppy, it's unit 0. Check with a local guru to find which value to use.
f tarfile	Specifies the name of the archive file. If the arch is on a disk or tape drive, the name is usually something like /dev/fd096 or /dev/tape.
filenames	Specifies the files you want to copy. If you specify directory names, all files and subdirectories in the directories are included.

Like disks, tapes can contain directories and subdirectories. You can extract all the files from a directory on a tape. To copy all the files from the /Report directory, for example, you can type

```
tar xvf /dev/tape /Report
```

If you use wildcard characters in the filename, be sure to enclose the entire thing in quotes, as shown in the following line, so that tar and the shell don't get confused:

```
tar xvf /dev/tape '/Report/*'
```

 For information about making and using backups, see the section "Call in the backup squad" in Chapter 23 of *UNIX For Dummies,* 2nd Edition.

Sample

Someone gives you a tape and tells you that it contains a file you want. The file is called something like mgmt.procedures, and the tape drive is named /dev/tape. To find out which files are on the tape, type

```
tar tvf /dev/tape
```

You see that a file is named manager.procedures. Assuming that it is the file you want, you copy it from the tape to the current working directory by typing

```
tar xvf /dev/tape manager.procedures
```

You can equally well use tar to create and unpack tar-format files, which are often used to pass around a bunch of files on networks. To put all the files in directory project in a tar-format file, type

```
tar cvf project.tar project
```

and to extract the files from a tar-format archive, type

```
tar xvf project.tar
```

tee

Copies text from a pipe into a file.

UNIXspeak

```
tee [-a] filenames
```

Option or Argument	Function
-a	Adds material to the end of the files instead of creating them.
filenames	Specifies the file (or files) to copy to.

`tee` is most useful for making a log of the output of a slow-running or long-running program while still seeing its output on-screen.

Sample

You're using the `find` command to find all your files that you haven't looked at for a month. You want to see the files on-screen as well as store the list of files in a new file named `stale.files`. Type

```
find . -atime +30 | tee stale.files
```

telnet

Lets you log in to a remote computer. Part VI explains how to use it.

tin

Lets you read messages posted to Usenet newsgroups. Part VIII explains how to use it.

time

Tells you how long a command took to run (from the time you pressed Enter or Return to the time you saw the next shell prompt).

UNIXspeak

```
time command [arguments]
```

Option or Argument	Function
command	Specifies the command or program you want to run.
arguments	Specifies the other information you have to type on the command line.

In the C shell, `time` with no arguments gives the times (elapsed and the amount of the computer's CPU you have used) since the shell began.

The `timex` command works the same way, except that it provides options for which information to display.

Sample

You are about to run your big, monthly analysis report, and you're curious as to how long it takes to run. You usually type this command to run it:

```
agdata 1994-oct
```

Instead, you use the time command to time it. Type

```
time agdata 1994-oct
```

After the report is finished running, you also see the elapsed time, execution time, and other information about how long the program took to run.

touch

Changes the date and time of a file without changing the file's contents.

UNIXspeak

```
touch [-a] [-c] [-m] [date] filenames
```

Option or Argument	Function
-a	Changes only the date and time the file was last accessed.
-c	Doesn't create files if they don't already exist. If you use touch without this option on a nonexistent filename, it creates an empty file.
-m	Changes only the date and time the file was last modified.
date	Specifies the date and time to give to the file (or files). The date and time must be in the format *mmddhhnn*, where *mm* is the month number, *dd* is the day number, *hh* is the hour (using a 24-hour clock), and *nn* is the minute.
filenames	Specifies the file (or files) whose date (or dates) and time (or times) you want changed.

If you leave out the date, touch changes the files' date and time to today, right now.

Sample

You are about to distribute a bunch of files to everyone in your department. Because you may distribute updates later, you would find it convenient if all the files had exactly the same modification date and time (the date and time the files were last modified). All the files are stored in the Distrib directory. To set the date and time to noon on Christmas, type

```
touch 12251200 Distrib/*
```

trn

Lets you read messages posted to Usenet newsgroups. Part VIII explains how to use it.

troff

A baroque but powerful text formatter, troff uses a complex formatting language to format text files for output on a high-quality printer or typesetter. (troff stands for *t*ypeset *run*off.)

UNIXspeak

```
troff [-mmacrofile] [-nfirstpage] [-opagelist]
    filenames
```

Option or Argument	Function
-mmacrofile	Specifies the file that contains macros used in the input file.
-nfirstpage	Uses *firstpage* as the page number of the first page that is printed.
-opagelist	Specifies the pages you want to print (3 , 6 , 15 , 21, for example).
filenames	Specifies the file (or files) that contains the input text.

Suppose that the paper jammed when it printed page 8, so you have to print it again. Type

```
troff -o8 report6 | lp
```

When someone gives you a text file formatted for troff, the printing instructions may say to use a particular *macro file* that contains macros used by troff. If so, you may need to tell troff about the macro when you run it. If you are told to use the ms macros, type

```
troff -ms report6 | lp
```

If you want to find out how to format text for use with troff (or its predecessor, nroff), *UNIX in a Nutshell* (O'Reilly & Associates) gives a useful overview.

Sample

Someone gives you a file that has been formatted for use with `troff` (that is, a text file that contains `troff` formatting codes, more properly called *requests* and *macros*). Luckily, you don't have to get into the world of `troff` formatting — you just have to print the file.

The file is called `report6`, and you usually use the `lp` command to print. Type

```
troff report6 | lp
```

tty

Displays the device name of your terminal.

UNIXspeak

```
tty
```

The terminal ID usually looks like the pathname of a subdirectory of the `/de` directory. Actually, `/de` is a directory (it stands for *de*vice) containing special files that are really connections to devices such as your terminal, printers, and tape drives.

 In case something goes wrong, knowing your terminal ID is a good idea. If you have to ask your local UNIX guru for help, he or she will probably ask for the terminal ID. Try to sound as though you know what you're talking about; know your terminal ID.

Sample

You need to know the name of your terminal so that you can report noise on the line to your system administrator. Type **tty**. You see

```
/dev/ttyd045
```

umask

Tells UNIX which permissions to give to files and directories.

UNIXspeak

```
umask [permissions]
```

Option or Argument	Function
permissions	Specifies the permissions to give to files you create. Unfortunately, you must specify the permissions as an octal number by using the method described below.

This table shows the numeric codes that make up a umask permission:

Number	Files You Create	Directories You Create
0	Read and write	List files, create files, and cd into directory
1	Read and write	List files and create files
2	Read only	List files and cd into directory
3	Read only	List files
4	Write only	Create files and cd into directory
5	Write only	Create files
6	No access	cd into directory
7	No access	No access

A umask permission consists of three of these numbers: the first, your own permissions; the second, those for your group; and the third, for everyone else. The first number in your umask permission should always be 0 (zero) so that you give yourself complete permissions for everything you create. The most common umasks are 022, which enable anyone to read the files, but only you can write them; 002, to let members of your group change your files and others only to read them; and 077, to let no one but you see any of your files.

You can always change the permissions for your files by using the chmod command, described earlier in this part.

Sample

Generally, when you create new files, you want everyone to be able to read the files, but you want only you and other members of your group to be able to write (edit) them. So you type

umask 002

When you create new files in the future, users who are not in your group can't edit the files.

unalias

Removes an alias name (C, BASH, and Korn shells only).

UNIXspeak

```
unalias names
```

Option or Argument	Function
names	Name (or names) of the aliases you want to delete.

See alias for more information about aliases. If you use the Bourne shell, you're out of luck because aliases don't exist there.

Sample

You created an alias for a directory you used frequently for a project. Now the project is over, and you don't want the alias anymore. Type

```
unalias projdir
```

uname

Tells you the name of the UNIX system you are using.

UNIXspeak

```
uname [-s][-a]
```

Option or Argument	Function
-s	Displays only the system name. If you don't use this option, you get a slew of other information (BSD only).
-a	Displays all system name info (System V only). Without this option, you get just the local system name.

To get the complete scoop about your system, type

```
uname
```

You see

```
plugh plugh 3.2.2 i386
```

You probably will have to ask a UNIX wizard to decode this message for you because it contains version numbers, CPU types, and other technical information.

Sample

You want to know the name of your UNIX system so that you can figure out your e-mail address. Type

```
uname -s
```

You see the name of the system.

uncompress

Restores a compressed file to its normal size.

UNIXspeak

```
uncompress [-c] filenames
```

Option or Argument	Function
-c	Displays the uncompressed version of the file but doesn't save it or delete the compressed file.
filenames	Specifies the compressed files to uncompress.

If you want to see what is in the compressed file facts, you can type

```
uncompress -c facts
```

You see the uncompressed contents of the file on-screen, but no new file is created, and the compressed file isn't deleted. You can use the zcat command to do the same thing.

To create a compressed file, *see* compress, earlier in this part. *See also* the pack and unpack commands.

Sample

Someone gives you a compressed file that contains information you want. The file is called facts.Z. The .Z at the end confirms that this file is compressed — if a filename ends with .z instead, it is packed, and you must use the unpack command instead. Type

```
uncompress facts
```

(You can leave the .Z off the filename because uncompress assumes that all compressed files have names that end with .Z.) uncompress creates a new file named facts that contains the uncompressed information from facts.Z. It also deletes facts.Z.

uniq

Removes repeated identical lines from a text file. If a file contains several adjacent lines that are the same, uniq deletes all but one.

UNIXspeak

```
uniq [-c] [-d] [-u] [-fields] [+chars] [existingfile
    [newfile]]
```

Option or Argument	Function
-c	Displays each line along with the number of times it occurs.
-d	Displays only lines that occur more than once.
-u	Displays only lines that the occur only once.
-fields	Skips the first *fields* fields on each line (fields are separated by either tabs or spaces) when you're comparing adjacent lines.
+chars	Skips the first *chars* characters on each line when you're comparing adjacent lines.
existingfile	Specifies the file that contains the input text.
newfile	Specifies the name to use for the new file that contains the output; if not specified, sends output to the standard output.

Suppose that you have a text file named visitors that contains a list of the people who used your corporate library this month. The file contains one name per line, with the date preceding each name. You want to know how many times each person visited the library. Type

```
sort visitors | uniq -1 -c > name.list
```

This command line sorts the visitors file so that identical lines are together. Then it runs the uniq command: It skips the first field on each line (the date) and counts the instances of each name. It stashes the output in a file named name.list.

Unless your file is already sorted, you should almost always use sort | uniq rather than just uniq.

Sample

You have an alphabetical list of the book titles in your corporate library, stored one per line in a text file named titles. You think that some titles may have been entered twice. To get rid of possible duplicates, type

```
uniq titles titles2
```

unpack

Restores a packed file to its original size.

UNIXspeak

unpack *filenames*

Option or Argument	Function
filenames	Specifies the packed files to unpack.

If you want to see what is in a packed file, you can use the pcat command to display its contents, like this:

pcat user.manual

You see the unpacked contents of the file on-screen, but no new file is created, and the packed file isn't deleted.

To create a packed file, see the pack command. *See also* the compress and uncompress commands.

Sample

Last year, you saved a file in packed format to save space. Now you want to use the file again. The file is called user.manual.z. The .z at the end confirms that this file is packed — if a filename ends with .Z (uppercase) instead, it is compressed, and you must use the uncompress command instead. Type

unpack user.manual.z

unpack creates a new file named user.manual that contains the unpacked information from user.manual.z. It also deletes user.manual.z.

uucp

Copies a file to another computer by using the old uucp system.

UNIXspeak

uucp [-m] *yourfile computer!newfile*

Option or Argument	Function
-m	Sends mail to you after the file has been copied.
yourfile	Specifies the name of your file on your own computer.
computer	Specifies the computer to which you want to copy the file.
newfile	Specifies the name to use on the other computer when you're creating the file.

You can specify where to store the file on the other computer, but uucp usually does not have permission to create files in any old directory. Instead, you may have to store it in uucp's own directory, like this:

```
uucp big.news carioca!~/big.news
```

Sample

You have a file named big.news that your friend is interested in. To send it to his computer, which is named carioca, type

```
uucp big.news carioca!big.news
```

uucp copies the file. If a transmission problem occurs, UNIX sends you electronic mail about it; otherwise, no news is good news.

If you use the C shell, be sure to type a backslash just before the exclamation point in the uucp command. Otherwise, the C shell interprets the exclamation point incorrectly.

uudecode

Converts a uuencoded file back into its original form.

UNIXspeak

```
uudecode filename
```

Option or Argument	Function
filename	Specifies the name of the uuencoded file.

uudecode says nothing when it runs unless something went wrong. You have to look at the input file yourself to find out the name of the file that it decoded.

Sample

A friend has sent you a uuencoded program by way of electronic mail. The message looks something like this:

```
begin 1746 run.me
LKJ3L409DFV13098D.V,,-F=0119208FH
""FLKJEO-19214309 ';'3;L46N-098ASD
```

By using your mail program (*see* Part V of this book), you save the message as a text file named uu.incoming. Then you decode the file by typing

```
uudecode uu.incoming
```

uudecode decodes the file and creates a file named run.me (the name to use for the decoded file is stored as part of the uuencoded file). You delete uu.incoming, which you don't want anymore, and try running the run.me program.

uuencode

Disguises a program as a text file so that you can send it through electronic mail or Usenet news.

UNIXspeak

uuencode *existingfile decodedname*

Option or Argument	Function
existingfile	Specifies the program (or other file) that you want to disguise as a text file.
decodedname	Specifies the name to be used later for the uudecoded file — after the file is mailed.

You can encode and mail your program in one fell swoop, like this:

```
uuencode fish.squish run.me | mail jordan@carioca
```

This command line uuencodes the file and mails it to your friend.

Sample

Your programming staff has written a fabulous new program you want to share with a few friends. The program is currently called fish.squish, but when your friends receive it, you want it to be called run.me. Type

```
uuencode fish.squish run.me > file.to.send
```

uuencode creates a uuencoded file named file.to.send, in which
the program has been transformed into a meaningless jumble of
letters, numbers, and punctuation. You send the file to your friends
via electronic mail. When they use uudecode (described earlier in
this part) on this file, it creates a file named run.me that contains the
runnable program.

Vacation

Automatically responds to incoming e-mail messages by telling
people that you are on vacation. (This command does not exist on all
UNIX systems.)

UNIXspeak

vacation [-1] [-m] [-M *filename*]

Option or Argument	Function
-l	Stores the names of people who send you messages while you are away. The names are stored in a file named .maillog in your home directory.
-m	Stores all the messages you received while you were away. The messages are stored in a file named .mailfile in your home directory.
-M *filename*	Sends the message in *filename* rather than the standard vacation message.

When you get back, cancel the vacation command by typing

mail -F ""

Doing so stops your mail from being forwarded to vacation.

Sample

You are about to go on your annual two-week pilgrimage to Fiji, and
you want people to know it. Type

vacation -m

Messages you receive are responded to automatically with a message
saying that you're away on vacation. The wording of the response
varies from one version of the vacation program to another.

vi

Runs a powerful screen-oriented text editor. *See* Part IV to learn how to use it.

wall

Displays a message on the screen of every single user on your entire computer network. Use with care!

UNIXspeak

wall

Don't use this command except for important news of universal interest. Otherwise, you will have angry office mates in a hurry.

Any user who turns off write messages with mesg n doesn't get wall messages either.

Sample

Three shopping bags of Chinese food arrive in the reception area of your company. It's lunchtime! Type

wall

UNIX says nothing. Type this message:

The Chinese food has arrived! Come to the meeting room!

Press Ctrl+D to end the message. Your message is immediately displayed on every terminal.

wais

Finds files stored on a network by searching for keywords you type. Part VII explains how to use it.

wc

Counts the number of words, lines, and characters in a file.

You can use wc to count the output of other commands. If you wonder, for example, how many files you have in your home directory and its subdirectories, you can type

find . -print | wc -w

This command finds all the files (beginning with the current directory) in the directory and its subdirectories. The output of the `find` command (the list of filenames) becomes the input to the `wc` command.

UNIXspeak

`wc [-c] [-l] [-w]` *filename*

Option or Argument	Function
-c	Displays only the number of characters in the file.
-l	Displays only the number of lines in the file.
-w	Displays only the number of words in the file.
filename	Specifies the name of the text file to count.

Sample

You spend two days working on an essay that is supposed to be no longer than 1,000 words. Type

`wc my.essay`

You see the number of characters, words, and lines in the file. If you want only the word count, type

`wc w my.essay`

who

Tells you who else is using this computer.

UNIXspeak

`who [-q] [am i]`

Option or Argument	Function
-q	Displays only usernames, not terminal IDs or other information.
am i	Displays your username, in case you have forgotten, or displays the username on any terminal that someone left logged in.

The users command displays a list of the users who are currently logged in. On some systems, you can type whoami (no spaces) rather than who am i to find out your username. *See also* the finger command to get more information about who is on your computer or on the network.

Sample

You wonder why your computer is so slow today. To find out who is using it, type

who

You see a list of usernames, terminal IDs, and login times.

Write

Displays a message on the screen of another user.

UNIXspeak

write *username* [*terminal*]

Option or Argument	Function
username	Specifies the person to whom you want to send a message.
terminal	Specifies the terminal the person is using. You have to mention this option only if the person is using several terminals (or terminal windows) at the same time.

Sometimes write tells you something like this:

```
dave is logged on more than one place
You are connected to "vt01".
Other locations are:
ttyp1
ttyp0
```

Which terminal is Dave using? In reality, Dave is probably using only one terminal and is probably using several xterm windows under Motif. Use the finger command to figure out which terminal is the one your friend is using.

See also talk and wall. Better yet, use e-mail (*see* Part V).

You can turn off write to their screen by using the mesg command.

Sample

You want to send an important message to your friend Dave, who works down the hall. Type

```
write dave
```

UNIX says nothing, so type the message and press Enter or Return at the end of each line:

```
Dave, it's Margy!
How about going out for some tacos?
```

At the end of the message, you press Ctrl+D. The message appears on Dave's screen.

xarchie

This Motif-based program looks for files stored on other computers by file name. Part VII explains how to use it.

Using Motif

Window managers are programs that control the way your screen is set up. Several managers are used on UNIX systems. Motif is by far the most popular, but others are still in use.

Only Motif is described in this part. If you're stuck with a window manager other than Motif, *see* Chapter 11 of *UNIX For Dummies,* 2nd Edition (IDG Books Worldwide, Inc.) for details.

In this part...

- ✓ Using the mouse to select and move stuff
- ✓ Opening, switching, moving, and resizing windows
- ✓ Doing mouse actions with keyboard shortcuts
- ✓ Exiting Motif

Changing the Window Size

You can change the size and shape of a window by using either the mouse or the keyboard.

With the mouse:

1. Move the mouse cursor to the window border.

2. Click and drag the border to make the window the size you want. The side borders move left and right, the top and bottom borders move up and down, and the corners move in all four directions.

Real mouse-haters use the keyboard:

1. Press Alt+F8 to put the window in "resize mode."

2. Press the arrow keys to change the window size. Holding down the Ctrl key while you press the arrow keys changes the size in larger increments.

3. Press Enter to accept the new size, or press Esc to return to the old size.

Exiting Motif

Exiting Motif means leaving the Motif window manager and returning to the UNIX shell. Depending on how your version of Motif is set up, you exit in one of two ways.

If you have a window called login:

1. Switch to that window. The window contains a UNIX shell.

2. Type **exit** or **logout** to exit the shell.

Otherwise:

1. Display the root menu by moving the mouse outside any window and pressing the right mouse button.

2. Choose the command on the root menu called Quit or Exit.

When you leave Motif, it terminates every program running in every window without saving your work. Clean up before you exit.

Keyboard Shortcuts

Keyboard shortcuts are the keyboard equivalents of mouse actions for the rodent-impaired who don't have a mouse or don't want to use it.

Key	Action
Alt+F1	Brings the window to the front, on top of all other windows.
Alt+F3	Drops the active window to the back, behind all other windows.
Alt+F4	Closes the active window.
Alt+F5	Restores an "iconified" window.
Alt+F6	Switches to the next window.
Alt+F7	Moves the active window.
Alt+F8	Changes the size of the active window.
Alt+F9	Minimizes the active window to an icon.
Alt+F10	Maximizes the active window to fill the screen.
Shift+Esc	Displays the window menu (described later in this part).
Alt+spacebar	Displays the window menu.
Alt+Tab	Switches to the next window.
Alt+Shift+Tab	Switches to the preceding window.

Your system administrator can change any or all of the keyboard and mouse commands. If you try some of these shortcuts and something unexpected happens, ask your system administrator for details.

If you're familiar with Microsoft Windows, you'll notice that these key combinations are about the same as the ones Windows uses.

Maximizing a Window

Maximizing a window means expanding it until it fills the entire screen. To maximize a window, do one of the following:

✦ Click its maximize button, the little block to the right of the minimize button.

✦ Choose Ma<u>x</u>imize from the window menu.

✦ Press Alt+F10.

Minimizing a Window

When you minimize a window, you shrink it to an icon, which is a little box on-screen that represents the window. From the icon, you can *restore* the window to its original state, with any running program just where it was when you minimized it. You can minimize a window in one of three ways:

✦ Click its minimize button, the little dot near the upper right.

✦ Choose Mi_n_imize from the window menu.

✦ Press Alt+F9.

Moving a Window

You can change the position of a window without changing its size. You can use the mouse, the keyboard, or both.

Using the mouse:

1. Move the mouse to the title area, the wide part of the top border that shows the name of the window.

2. Press and hold down the mouse button.

3. Drag the window to where you want it.

4. Release the button.

Using the keyboard:

1. Press Alt+F7 to put the window in "move mode."

2. Press the cursor keys to move the window. Holding down the Ctrl key while using the cursor keys moves the window in larger increments.

3. Press Enter to accept the new position, or press Esc to return to the old place.

You can move a window off the edge of the screen if you want to get it out of the way for a minute.

Opening Windows in a User-Friendly Way

1. Move the mouse to a part of the screen outside any window.

2. Press the right mouse button. If you have large windows, you may have to move one to clear some screen area. When you press the mouse button, a "root" menu appears. With luck, it has an entry for the menu you want.

Several user-friendly shell programs also provide icons for popular programs; if you have one of these programs, click the appropriate icon.

Opening a Window in an Obsolete but Easy Way

1. Switch to a window running the UNIX shell.

2. Type as a UNIX command the name of the program you want to run.

Restoring a Window

When you restore a window, you return it to its previous size. To restore a window do one of the following:

✦ Click the maximize button again.

✦ Choose <u>R</u>estore from the window menu.

✦ Press Alt+F5.

Restoring a Window from an Icon

You restore a window from an icon by expanding the icon back to the window that appeared before you "iconized" it. You must restore a window before you can use the program. Use one of these three ways:

✦ From the icon's window menu, choose <u>R</u>estore.

✦ Double-click the icon with the left mouse button.

✦ Move to the icon and press Alt+F5.

Selecting Several Things

You can select many items in an area, such as a chunk of text in a window.

1. Move the cursor to the beginning of the area you want to select.

2. Press the left mouse button and hold it down.

3. While keeping the mouse button pressed, move the cursor to the end of what you want to select. The selected material changes color as you do this step.

4. Release the mouse button.

Switching Windows

When you switch windows, you select which window is the *active* window, the window that receives text you type from the keyboard. Motif makes the border around the active window a different color from the others. Depending on your setup, you use one of these methods to switch windows:

✦ **Click-to-type:** Move the mouse to the window you want and click the mouse anywhere in that window.

✦ **Move-to-type:** Although it's not standard Motif (but quite popular), you merely move the mouse to the window you want to use.

To tell which way you can select a window, move your mouse from one window to another without clicking. If the window borders change colors, you have move-to-type. If not, you have click-to-type.

You can bring any window to the front (that is, make it so that no other overlapping window obscures it) by clicking anywhere in the window's frame or by moving to the window and pressing Alt+F1.

Window Anatomy

Each Motif window is surrounded by a border that contains lots of exciting pieces, as the following figure shows:

The following table explains what the parts of the window border do.

Name	Use
Window menu	Displays the window menu.
Title bar	Moves the window, resizes it, and so on.
Minimize	Turns the window into an icon.
Maximize	Makes the window fill the screen.
Resize border	Changes the size of the window.

The Window Menu

In the window menu, you perform standard window operations, such as changing the size of the window, moving the window, and minimizing the window to an icon. You can display the window menu in one of three ways:

✦ Click the little bar in the upper-left corner with the left mouse button.

✦ Click anywhere in the window border with the middle mouse button.

✦ Press Shift+Esc or Alt+spacebar.

Restore	Alt+F5
Front	Alt+F1
Move	Alt+F7
Size	Alt+F8
Minimize	Alt+F9
Maximize	Alt+F10
Lower	Alt+F3
Close	Alt+F4

The window menu lists the most common window operations along with their shortcut keys. Operations that aren't currently valid are grayed out. You can select any of the menu entries in three ways:

✦ Click the menu entry with the mouse.

✦ Type the underlined letter in the menu entry.

✦ Press the shortcut key combination.

TIP

Icons (*see* the "Restoring a Window from an Icon" section, earlier in this part) have window menus also, which you display in the much the same way: Click the icon with the left mouse button; click and hold the middle mouse button; or press Shift+Esc or Alt+spacebar.

You can always use the shortcut key combination regardless of whether the window menu is displayed. If you do a great deal of window wrangling, the shortcut keys are the easiest way to do many window operations.

You can display the window menu and select an entry in one fell swoop:

1. Move the cursor to the bar in the upper-left corner and press and hold down the left mouse button.

2. When the menu appears, move the cursor to the entry you want and release the button.

This menu, known as a *pull-down menu,* is used in lots of applications, including Motif.

Using Text Editors (ed, vi, emacs, and pico)

Text editors let you write and save messages, such as e-mail messages.

Text editors do not have the advanced functions you might find in word processors. However, you can easily read files created with these programs and send files created with text editors over a network.

In this part...

- ✔ Using ed, an old-fashioned, simple line editor
- ✔ Using vi, a more sophisticated, screen-based editor found on almost all systems
- ✔ Using emacs, a powerful, full-featured, screen-based editor
- ✔ Using pico, an easy-to-use, screen-based editor

Using the ed Text Editor

ed is an old-fashioned line editor used to edit text files, such as writing electronic-mail messages or shell scripts. Because screen editors are much easier to use (*see* vi, emacs, and pico, later in this part), use ed only if other editors are not available on your system.

Starting ed

To start ed, simply type **ed**.

To create a new file and give it a name, or to load an existing file, type

ed *filename*

If the file already exists, you see the number of characters in it. If you are creating a new file, you see a question mark.

To complicate matters, ed is always in either *command mode* or *input mode*. In command mode, letters you type are interpreted as commands. In input mode, what you type is entered in the file you are editing.

To make ed more usable, press P to put it in *prompt mode* so that it displays an asterisk whenever it is in command mode and waiting for a command. Then press H to tell ed to display more helpful messages when something goes wrong.

Getting out of ed

1. If you are in input mode, type a period and press Enter to go to command mode.

2. Press w to save your work (unless you don't want to).

3. Press q to quit the program. You see the shell prompt again.

If you want to exit ed without saving changes you made to the file, press q. When ed displays a question mark, press q again.

ed commands

All ed commands consist of one letter. Be sure to use the same capitalization shown in this section — most basic ed commands are lowercase.

ed commands work with one line at a time. The line you are presently using is called the *current line,* and commands apply to that line unless you say otherwise.

Command	What It Does
a	Appends text (that is, adds a line after the current line and switches to input mode). To exit input mode and return to command mode, type a period on a line by itself.
*n*a	Appends text after line number *n*.
d	Deletes current line.
*n*d	Deletes line number *n*.
*n,m*d	Deletes lines numbered *n* through *m*.
h	Displays a help message right now.
H	Displays help messages whenever anything goes wrong.
i	Inserts text (that is, inserts a line before the current line and switches to input mode). To exit input mode and return to command mode, type a period on a line by itself.
*n*i	Inserts text before line number *n*.
n	Displays the current line with a line number.
*n,m*n	Displays lines numbered *n* through *m* with line numbers.
1,$n	Displays all the lines in the file with line numbers.
p	Displays the current line without line numbers (we recommend using the n command instead because you have to know line numbers to edit the lines).
*n,m*p	Displays lines numbered *n* through *m* without line numbers.
1,$p	Displays all the lines in the file without line numbers.
P	Displays an asterisk whenever ed is in command mode.
q	Quits the program.
Q	Quits even if changes haven't been saved.
s/*text1*/*text2*/	Substitutes *text2* for *text1* the first place it appears in the current line.
*n,m*s/*text1*/*text2*/	Substitutes *text2* for *text1* the first place it appears in each line numbered *n* through *m*.
u	Undoes the last change you made.
w	Writes (saves) the file.
Enter (or Return)	Displays the next line of the file.
. (period)	Displays the next line of the file. In input mode, typing a period on a line by itself returns you to command mode.

There are lots of other ed commands — almost every letter is a command. Be careful what you type while you are in command mode!

Using the vi Text Editor

vi is a widely-used, powerful screen editor based on ed that is available on almost all systems. You use it to edit text files, including writing e-mail messages or shell scripts.

Starting vi

To start vi, simply type **vi**.

To create a new file and give it a name, or to load an existing file, type

vi *filename*

vi displays the first screen of the file. If the file isn't long enough to fill the screen, vi shows tildes (~) on the blank lines. The cursor is at the beginning of the file.

vi is always in either *command mode* or *input mode* (also called *insert mode*). In command mode, letters you type are interpreted as commands. In input mode, what you type is entered in the file you are editing.

To switch from command mode to input mode, use an a or i command (described later in this part) to tell vi where to put the new text.

To switch from input mode to command mode, press the Esc key. Press it a few times, just to be sure. (vi just beeps when you press Esc when you are already in command mode.)

To run a friendlier version of vi, try typing **vedit**. The vedit program displays various helpful messages, including messages that tell you when you are in input or command mode.

Getting out of vi

1. If you are in input mode, press the Esc key to get into command mode.

2. Type **:w** to save your work (unless you don't want to).

3. Type **ZZ** to quit the program (those are capital Zs).

If you want to exit vi without saving the changes you have made to the file, type **q!** to quit without saving.

vi commands

Most vi commands are one letter. Be sure to use either capital or small letters as shown — in many cases, a capital letter does something rather different from the same small letter!

Command	What It Does
Esc	Returns to command mode from input mode. In command mode, it just beeps.
Enter	Moves the cursor to the beginning of the next line.
0 (zero)	Moves the cursor to the beginning of the current line.
$	Moves the cursor to the end of the current line.
+	Moves the cursor to the beginning of the next line.
-	Moves the cursor to the beginning of the preceding line.
)	Moves the cursor to the beginning of the next sentence. (A sentence ends with a period, exclamation point, or question mark followed by two spaces.)
(	Moves the cursor to the beginning of the current sentence.
}	Moves the cursor to the beginning of the next paragraph. (A paragraph ends with a blank line.)
{	Moves the cursor to the beginning of the current paragraph.
/text	Searches forward through the file for the text.
/	Repeats the same search, searching forward.
?	Repeats the same search, searching backward.
:!command	Runs a shell command and then returns to v i .
a	Adds text (that is, switches to input mode so that the text you type is added immediately after the cursor).
A	Adds text at the end of the current line, switching to input mode.
b or B	Moves the cursor backward one word.
dd	Deletes the entire current line.
ndd	Deletes the next n lines.
D	Deletes the text from the cursor to the end of the line.
d ^	Deletes the text from the cursor to the beginning of the line.
dw	Deletes the next word.
d)	Deletes to the end of the sentence.
d}	Deletes to the end of the paragraph.
dG	Deletes to the end of the file. (Watch out!)
e or E	Moves the cursor to the end of the word.
G	Goes (moves the cursor) to the end of the file.
1G	Moves the cursor to the beginning of the file.
h	Moves the cursor left one character.
H	Moves the cursor to the top line of the screen.

(continued)

Command	What It Does
i	Inserts text (that is, switches to input mode so that the text you type is inserted immediately before the cursor).
I	Inserts text at the beginning of the current line, switching to input mode.
j	Moves the cursor down one line.
k	Moves the cursor up one line.
l	Moves the cursor right one character.
L	Moves the cursor to the bottom line of the screen.
n	Repeats the last search (made with /).
N	Repeats the last search (made with /), searching in the opposite direction.
o	Opens (creates) a new line after the current line, switching to input mode so that you can type text on it.
O (the letter)	Opens a new line before the current line, switching to input mode so that you can type text on it.
p	Inserts ("puts") text deleted by the last y or Y command. The text is added just after the cursor.
P	Inserts text deleted by the last y or Y command, just before the cursor.
:q! (followed by Enter)	Exits from the program without saving your changes.
R	Replaces text, switching to input mode so that the text you type replaces the text that is currently to the right of the cursor (also called *overtype* mode).
:sh	Runs the shell while putting v i on hold. To return from the shell, type **exit** or press Ctrl+D. You return to v i with the same file loaded and your cursor in the same position. Be sure to save your file before trying this command.
u	Undoes the last change.
U	Undoes all changes to the current line since you moved to it.
w or W	Moves the cursor forward one word.
:w (followed by Enter)	Writes (saves) the file.
x	Deletes the character to the right of the cursor.
X	Deletes the character to the left of the cursor.
:x (followed by Enter)	Exits v i and saves any changes to the file.
nx	Deletes the next n characters.
nX	Deletes the previous n characters.

Command	What It Does
yy or Y	Copies ("yanks") the current line to a buffer for later use. Deletes the line from the file.
yw	Copies the current word to a buffer for later use and deletes the word from the file.
y)	Copies the current sentence to a buffer for later use and deletes the sentence from the file.
y}	Copies the current paragraph to a buffer for later use and deletes the paragraph from the file.
ZZ	Exits from vi and saves any changes to the file.
Ctrl+A	Suspends vi and returns to the UNIX shell. Works only if your UNIX shell handles job control. Resume vi by typing **fg**.
Ctrl+B	Scrolls backward one screen.
Ctrl+F	Scrolls forward one screen.
:ed command	You can do any ed command in vi by typing a colon and the ed command and then pressing Enter.

There are lots of other vi commands — almost every letter is a command. Be careful what you type while you are in command mode! And be sure to use capital and small letters in commands just as they are listed in the table.

vi commands in input mode

Command	What It Does
Esc	Returns to command mode from input mode (Ctrl+C does this too).
Ctrl+B	Scrolls backward one screen.
Ctrl+F	Scrolls forward one screen.
Ctrl+H	Backspaces.
Ctrl+J	Moves the cursor down one line (Ctrl+N also does this).
Ctrl+L	Redisplays the text on the screen (Ctrl+R also does this).
Ctrl+P	Moves the cursor up one line.
Ctrl+W	Moves the cursor backward to the beginning of the word.

Using the emacs Text Editor

emacs is a powerful screen editor that lets you edit multiple files at one time.

Starting emacs

To start emacs, simply type **emacs**. To create a new file and give it a name, or to load an existing file, type

emacs *filename*

emacs displays the first screen of the file. The cursor is at the beginning of the file.

On some systems, the emacs program is named e or gmacs or epsilon. Some UNIX installations don't have emacs. (But they should.)

Getting out of emacs

1. Save your work by pressing Ctrl+x, Ctrl+s.

2. Exit emacs by pressing Ctrl+x, Ctrl+c. You see the shell prompt.

emacs commands

You type commands by using various combinations of the Ctrl and Meta keys. Unfortunately, your keyboard probably does not have a key marked Meta, so press the Alt key instead. If you don't have an Alt key, press the Esc key and then the key it modifies.

Command	What It Does
Meta+< (that is, Meta+ Shift+comma)	Moves the cursor to the beginning of the file.
Meta+>	Moves the cursor to the end of the file.
Meta+%	Replaces all occurrences of one piece of text with another. emacs asks you for the text to be replaced and the text to replace it with.
Ctrl+@ (that is, Ctrl+Shift+2)	Puts a *mark* at the cursor location. After you move the cursor, you can move or copy the text between the mark and the cursor by using the Ctrl+w or Meta+w keystroke.
Ctrl+a	Moves the cursor to the beginning of the line.
Ctrl+b	Moves the cursor back one character.
Meta+b	Moves the cursor back one word.
Ctrl+d	Deletes the character to the right of the cursor.
Meta+d	Deletes the current word.
Ctrl+e	Moves the cursor to the end of the line.
Ctrl+f	Moves the cursor forward one character.

Command	What It Does
Meta+f	Moves the cursor forward one word.
Ctrl+g	Cancels the current command.
Ctrl+h	Enters the online help system.
Ctrl+h c	Displays the command that runs when you press a particular key.
Ctrl+h t	Runs a tutorial about emacs.
Ctrl+k	Deletes ("kills") the text from the cursor to the end of the line and stores it in the *kill buffer*.
Ctrl+n	Moves the cursor to the next line.
Ctrl+p	Moves the cursor to the preceding line.
Meta+q	Reformats the current paragraph, using word wrap, so that the lines are full.
Ctrl+s	Searches for text. When you find what you are looking for, press Esc or move the cursor. To repeat the search, press Ctrl+s again.
Meta+s	Centers the current line.
Ctrl+t	Transposes the two characters before the cursor.
Meta+t	Transposes the two words before the cursor.
Meta+u	Capitalizes all the letters of the current word.
Ctrl+v	Scrolls down one screen.
Meta+v	Scrolls up one screen.
Ctrl+w	Deletes ("whomps") the text between the mark (set by using Ctrl I @) and the cursor and stores it in the kill buffer. To get it back, press Ctrl+y.
Meta+w	Copies the text between the mark and the cursor to the kill buffer so that you can insert copies of it by using Ctrl+y.
Ctrl+x Ctrl+c	Exits emacs.
Ctrl+x Ctrl+s	Saves the file.
Ctrl+x Ctrl+u	Undoes the last change.
Meta+x doctor (followed by Enter)	Stops doing useful work and starts "doctor mode," playing a game in which emacs responds to your statements with questions. Save your work first. Not in all versions of emacs support this mode.
Ctrl+y	Inserts ("yanks") the text that is in the kill buffer and places it after the cursor.
Del (the Del key)	Deletes the character before the cursor.
Meta+Del	Deletes the word in front of the cursor.

emacs commands for editing multiple files

These commands are used for editing several files at the same time and for viewing several files on-screen. Each file is edited in an emacs *buffer* and is visible in a *window*.

Command	What It Does
Ctrl+x b	Switches to a different buffer for editing.
Ctrl+x Ctrl+f	Finds a file and reads it into a buffer for editing.
Ctrl+x k	Closes this buffer. If you haven't saved the file, emacs asks whether you want to save the file.
Ctrl+x Ctrl+i	Inserts a file into the current file at the cursor position.
Ctrl+x o	Switches to the other window.
Ctrl+x Ctrl+s	Saves the current buffer into its file.
Ctrl+x 1	Unsplits the screen so that only one window is visible. This command doesn't close any buffers.
Ctrl+x 2	Splits the screen into two windows so that you can view two files at once.

Using the pico Text Editor

pico is a simple, easy-to-use text editor. Commands are listed at the bottom of the screen as a reference.

pico is relatively new and may not be available on some systems. If it is, use it — because it's easy!

Starting pico

To start pico, simply type **pico**.

To create a new file and give it a name or to load an existing file, type

pico *filename*

pico displays the first screen of the file. The cursor is at the beginning of the file.

Getting out of pico

1. Press Ctrl+x.

2. pico prompts you to save your work. Press y to save or n to exit without saving.

pico commands

You type commands by holding down the Control (Ctrl) key and pressing a letter.

The following commands are available in `pico`. The corresponding function key commands are shown in parentheses.

Command	What It Does
Ctrl+g (F1)	Displays the help screen.
Ctrl+f	Moves the cursor forward a character.
Ctrl+b	Moves the cursor backward a character.
Ctrl+p	Moves the cursor to the preceding line.
Ctrl+n	Moves the cursor to the next line.
Ctrl+a	Moves the cursor to the beginning of the current line.
Ctrl+e	Moves the cursor to the end of the current line.
Ctrl+v (F8)	Moves the cursor forward a page of text.
Ctrl+y (F7)	Moves the cursor backward a page of text.
Ctrl+w (F6)	Searches for text within the file.
Ctrl+l	Refreshes the display.
Ctrl+d	Deletes the character immediately to the right of the cursor.
Ctrl+k (F9)	Cuts the line of text at the cursor position.
Ctrl+u (F10)	Uncuts (pastes) text, inserting it at the cursor position.
Ctrl+il	Inserts a tab at the cursor position.
Ctrl+j (F4)	Displays the current paragraph as justified text.
Ctrl+t (F12)	Runs the spelling checker.
Ctrl+c (F11)	Displays the number of lines of text that exist.
Ctrl+r (F5)	Inserts ("reads") an existing file at the cursor position.
Ctrl+o (F3)	Saves ("outputs") the text to a file.
Ctrl+x (F2)	Exits `pico`, prompting you to save the file.

The online `pico` help screens display the ^ character to represent the Ctrl key. The online help also displays capital letters in commands. Therefore, if the help screen tells you to type **^B**, you should hold down the Ctrl key and press b.

See also *UNIX For Dummies,* 2nd Edition (IDG Books Worldwide, Inc.), Chapter 13, and *MORE UNIX For Dummies* (IDG Books Worldwide, Inc.), Chapters 11 and 12 for more information about `vi`, `emacs`, and `pico`.

Sending and Receiving Electronic Mail

Every UNIX system comes with some sort of mail system. At worst, you have a primitive mail program and can send mail only to other users on your machine. At best, you use a much better mail program (probably elm, Pine, or xmail) and can send mail to anyone on the Internet.

In this part...

 ✔ Using Mail, the basic mail program that comes with most UNIX systems

 ✔ Using elm, the most popular screen-based mail program

 ✔ Using Pine, an easy-to-use, full-featured mail program

 ✔ Using xmail, a graphical, Motif-based mail program

For each program, we will show you how to send, read, and save mail.

Addressing Your Mail

When you address your mail, you enter the *mail address* of the person to whom you want to send mail.

Every user has a mail address, usually the same as the user (login) name. If your computer is attached to a network, your mail address is your user name, an at sign (@), and the name of your computer— betsy@marketing, for example.

Some systems that run the ancient uucp network software use an exclamation point, as in marketing!betsy. System administrators can set up other mail addresses for mailing lists, remote users, and other purposes.

Mail

Mail is the basic mail program that comes with all UNIX systems. It may be named mail, or it might be called mailx or Mail. You use the same program to send and receive mail, with different arguments.

If your system has mailx or Mail, there may be another, even older mail program you don't want to use.

In our examples, we use the Mail program; substitute **mail** or **mailx** if you use them.

Sending a message

1. Run your mail program and give it the name (or names) of the mail recipients, like this:

Mail elvis@ntw.org

2. Depending on how the mail program is configured, it may prompt you for a subject line; if so, type one:

Subject: Hound dogs

If it doesn't ask for a subject and you want to provide one, type **~s** followed by the subject:

~sHound dogs

3. Type your message.

4. When you're finished entering the text of the message, type a period on a line by itself. The mail program responds with EOT. (Some ancient versions don't understand the period; for them, press Ctrl+D.) UNIX sends the message.

While you're sending mail, the editing commands in the following table are available. You start each command with a tilde (~) on a new, blank line.

Command	What It Does
~b *name*	Adds a name to the blind carbon copy list.
~c *name*	Adds a name to the carbon copy list.
~e	Runs a text editor (usually v i) to edit the message.
~f	Forwards the current message from the mailbox to someone else.
~p	Prints (displays on-screen) the message so far.
~q	Quits and abandons this message.
~r *file*	Reads in the contents of *file*.
~s *subject*	Sets the message subject.
~c *name*	Adds *name* to the list of recipients.
~v	Visual edit: runs the v i editor so that you can edit the message.
~w *file*	Writes the current message to a file.
~.	Ends the message and delivers it.

TIP

If you want to save a copy of a message you are sending, include your own user name in the blind carbon copy list by using the ~b command.

Reading your messages

1. Run your mail program by typing **Mail**, **mail**, or **mailx**. The mail program shows you your new messages followed by a question mark prompt, like this:

```
mailx version 3.1  Type ? for help.
"/usr/mail/johnl": 21 messages 1 new
>N 21 elvis Thu Dec 16 15:59   17/361
Club date?
```

2. To read each new message, press Enter.

3. After reading a message, decide whether you want to save it. To delete it, press d, or type **dp** to delete it and display the next message. To keep the message and display the next, press Enter.

Forwarding a message

To send a copy of an incoming message to a third party:

1. After you read a message, press m to tell the program that you want to create a new message.

2. Type the address to which you want to forward the message.

3. Enter an appropriate subject when asked.

4. Type ~**m** on a separate line to insert the original message into the mail you are sending.

5. Enter more text if you want to, and then type a period on a separate line or press Ctrl+D to finish.

Printing a message

The Mail program doesn't have a built-in printing command, but you can tell it to send the message to the standard printing program. Within the Mail program on BSD UNIX systems, type this line:

```
| lpr
```

(That's a vertical bar, a space, and the lpr command.)

On UNIX System V, type this line:

```
| lp
```

Saving a message

With Mail, you can store messages in a text file for later perusing, editing, printing, or other uses. To save a message, follow these steps:

1. Run your mail program. It shows you your new messages.

2. Select the message you want either by pressing Enter until the message you want appears or by typing the message number and then pressing Enter.

3. Type **s**, a space, and the name of the file in which to save the message.

You can save as many messages as you want in a single file. That file can be treated as a mailbox; use Mail -f filename to tell Mail to read its contents.

Exiting the mail program

Press q to quit and save changes to your mailbox.

Press x to exit and discard changes to your mailbox.

Command line options

```
mail [-e] [-f file] [-N] [-H] [-s subject] [recipients]
```

Option or Argument	Function
-e	Tells you whether there's any new mail, without displaying it.
-f file	Reads your mail from the mailbox file you specify.
-N	Doesn't list message headers when it starts.
-H	Lists only the messages headers and then exits.
-s subject	Sets the subject when sending mail.
recipients	Sets the name (or names) of the recipient (or recipients) when you're sending mail.

elm

To run the program, type **elm**. You see the *message index,* a nice listing of your messages with one message per line. At the bottom of the screen is a list of the elm commands you can use.

See also UNIX For Dummies, 2nd Edition, Chapter 19, and MORE UNIX For Dummies, Chapter 18.

Sending a message

1. Type **elm**.

2. Press m.

3. elm asks who to send the message to. Type a mail address.

4. elm prompts you for the message subject. Enter one.

5. elm may ask for addresses to which you want to send copies of the message. Type the names if you want to include any. (Type your own user name if you want to keep a copy for yourself.) Just press Enter or Return if you don't want to send any copies.

6. elm runs a text editor, usually vi. Type your message.

7. After completing your message, give the commands to save the completed message and exit the editor. In vi, type **ZZ** or **:x**. In emacs, press Ctrl+X, Ctrl+S, Ctrl+X, Ctrl+C.

elm asks something like this:

```
Please choose one of the following options by
    parenthesized letter:
e)dit message, !)shell, h)eaders, c)opy file, s)end,
    or f)orget.
```

You have the choice of pressing s to send the message, h to edit the header lines, e to go back and edit the message some more, c to copy a file into the message, ! to run a shell command, or f to forget it and throw away the message.

8. To send the message, press s. elm sends the message and displays the list of messages in your mailbox again.

TIP

If you would rather use emacs or pico instead of vi as your text editor, ask your system administrator to set up elm to run that editor, or see the section "Changing your elm options" at the end of this section.

Reading your messages

1. Type **elm**. You see the message index.

2. Press the cursor keys to move the cursor to the message you want. If the message is off the bottom of the screen (because you have more messages than can fit, you popular person), press the spacebar to see each subsequent screen of messages or use the cursor keys to scroll through the list.

3. Press Enter to view the message. If the message is too long to fit on-screen, press the spacebar to see more of it.

4. When you finish reading the message, decide whether you want to keep it. Press d to delete the message and go on to the next one. To keep it, press the up- or down-arrow keys to go to preceding or subsequent messages without deleting anything.

5. To stop reading messages, press i to return to the message index.

Printing a message

This task prints the message on a printer connected to the UNIX system. If you dial in from a PC, this process won't do what you want — instead, you have to save the message to a file, download the file, and then print the downloaded file.

1. Type **elm**. You see the message index.

2. Press the cursor keys to select the message you want to print.

3. Press p. The message is printed.

Saving a message

You can use elm to store messages in a text file for later perusing, editing, printing, or other uses.

1. Type **elm**. You see the message index.

2. Press the cursor keys to select the message you want to save.

3. Press s.

4. Type the name of the file in which to save the message, or press Enter to accept elm's suggested filename (usually the name of the sender).

 Your mailbox usually resides in a subdirectory of your home directory called Mail. If you precede a filename with an equal sign, such as -loveletters, elm puts the file in your Mail directory. You can save multiple messages into one file; elm just adds the new messages to the end of the file.

Exiting the program

To quit elm and save any changes you have made to your mailbox, such as deleting messages:

1. Press q.

2. elm asks whether you want to save the messages you've already read. Press y or Enter to save them in a file named received, or press n to leave them in your mailbox. Either way, your messages are saved in one place or the other.

To quit elm without saving changes to your mailbox:

1. Press x.

2. If you've made changes, elm asks whether you really want to exit without saving them.

3. Press y to exit without saving or n if you change your mind.

Changing your elm options

You can customize elm so that it uses the editor you like, displays messages in the order you want, and other things. To customize, follow these steps:

1. Type **elm**. You see the message index.

2. To see your elm options, press o. elm displays a list of its options, along with your setting for each one. You should leave most of these settings alone so that you don't break elm.

3. To use a different editor for composing messages, press e. Your cursor jumps to the name of the editor that elm currently runs when you want to send a message. Edit this program name and press Enter. Notice that it is a full pathname; ask your system administrator to tell you the full pathname of the editor you want to use. Then press Enter.

4. To change the order in which messages are displayed in the message index, press s. Then press the spacebar repeatedly until you see the ordering you want. Press r to switch between forward and reverse orders. (Our favorite is Date Mail Sent, sorting from least recent to most recent.) Then press Enter.

5. To change other settings, press the letter that appears in front of the parenthesis at the beginning of its line. Make the change and press Enter.

6. When you finish messing around with the options, type > to save your changes. If you think that you may have made a mistake, skip this step.

7. To return to your elm message index, press i.

Getting help

To see online help in elm, type ?. Typing another question mark displays a list of all the commands.

Command line options

```
elm [-f file] [-h] [-s subject] -v [recipients]
```

Option or Argument	Function
-f file	Reads mail from *file* rather than from your usual mailbox.
-h	Displays help about the elm program.
-s subject	Sets the subject when sending mail (applies only if you also specify a recipient for sending mail without first seeing the message index).
-v	Reports elm's version number.
recipients	Sets the name (or names) of the recipient (or recipients) when you're sending mail. This option is for sending mail without first seeing the message index.

Pine

Pine is an easy-to-use, menu-driven mail program. It uses folders to store incoming mail and addresses. It also lets you send attachments, which are non-text files such as graphics files or spreadsheets.

To start Pine, type **pine**. You see the *Main menu*. At the bottom of the screen is a list of Pine commands you can use.

Command	What It Does
?	Shows the help screen.
C	Composes and sends a message.
I	Displays messages in the current folder.
L	Selects a folder to view.
A	Creates or modifies address books.
S	Accesses setup options.
Q	Quits Pine.
O	Shows all other available commands.
P	Selects the preceding item displayed on the menu.
N	Selects the next item displayed on the menu.
R	Displays release notes, which contain information for using Pine.
K	Locks the keyboard, preventing others from accessing it when you are not at your computer.
G	Goes to a specified folder.

See also Chapter 19 of *UNIX For Dummies*, 2nd Edition, and Chapter 18 of *MORE UNIX For Dummies*

Sending a message

1. Type **pine**.

2. Press c (for compose) to display the Compose Message screen.

3. In the Address field, type a mail address and press Enter. You can type several names if desired, with a comma separating them.

4. In the Cc: field, enter the addresses of other people you want to receive the message. Press Enter.

5. The Attachment field lets you send a file that is not a text file (such as a graphics file or word processing document). Enter the pathname of the file here (if the file is in your home directory, you can just type the filename). Then press Enter.

6. In the Subject field, briefly describe the message and press Enter.

7. Type your message. Pine uses the pico editor described in Part IV. If you want to send a file that you previously wrote, press Ctrl+R to read in a file. Enter the pathname of the file here (if the file is in your home directory, you can just type the filename).

8. To send your message, press Ctrl+X.

Pine asks:

Send message?

9. Press y (for *yes*) or Enter. The message is sent, and a copy of it is saved in the sent mail folder.

Reading your messages

New messages are stored in the INBOX folder. To read them:

1. Type **pine**. The Main menu appears.

2. At the Main menu, press i (for *index*). A list of mail messages appears.

3. Use the arrow keys to highlight the message you want to view, or press p or n to move up or down a message. Press v (for View) or Enter to read a selected message.

4. To return to the index, press i (for *index*).

The left side of the INBOX screen shows the status of the messages as follows:

N	The message is new.
+	The message was sent directly to you (it was not forwarded).
D	You have read the message and it has been marked for deletion.
A	You responded to this message by using the Reply feature.

Replying to a message

To reply to a message you are reading, follow these steps:

1. Press r (for *reply*).

You are asked whether you want to include the original message in your reply. Also, if the original message was sent to more than one person, you are asked whether you want to reply to all recipients.

2. To send your message, press Ctrl+X.

Pine asks:

Send message?

3. Press y (for *yes*) or Enter.

Forwarding a message

To forward a message that you have selected at the Index screen or that you are viewing, follow these steps:

1. Press f (for Forward). A copy of the message opens and the To: field is highlighted.

2. Enter the address of your recipient and send the message as usual. Note that you can modify the original message if you wish.

Printing a message

To print messages from either the Folder Index screen or the View Message screen, press y.

Pine provides three options for printing. Do not change these settings if you can print successfully.

To choose the printing method that Pine uses, follow these steps:

1. At the Pine Main menu, press s (for *setup*).

2. Press p (for *printer*).

Pine displays three options:

- PC and Macintosh printing
- UNIX printing
- A custom print command

3. Enter **1**, **2**, or **3** to select one of the three printing methods. You may be required to enter a command that will be used to access the printer.

Saving a message

When you save a message, you can store it in the saved messages folder, or you can specify another folder:

1. On the Index menu, use the arrow keys or press p or n to highlight the message you want to save.

2. Press s (for *save*) to save the message. You can also press e (for *export*) to save the message to a file in your home directory.

3. If you press s, you are asked whether you want to save the message to the saved messages folder, which is the default. If you want to save the message to the default folder, press Enter. If you would rather save the message to another folder, enter the name of the folder and then press Enter.

Once you save a message, the message in the INBOX folder is automatically marked for deletion. When you quit Pine, you are asked whether you want to permanently delete the message from the INBOX folder.

Deleting a message

Pine lets you delete and undelete messages. To mark for deletion a message you do not want, follow these steps:

1. On the Folder Index screen, use the arrow keys or press p or n to highlight the message you want to delete. If you read the message, it is automatically marked for deletion.

2. Press d (for *delete*).

3. If you change your mind about a message that you have marked for deletion, press u (for *undelete*) to restore the message.

A message that is marked for deletion will not be deleted until you "expunge" it, or permanently delete it. To expunge a message, follow these steps:

1. On the Folder Index screen, press x (for *expunge*).

Pine asks:

```
Expunge message(s)"?
```

2. Press y or the Enter key.

Adding an address to an address book

Pine lets you store the addresses of individuals or groups of people that you can then easily retrieve when you write new messages:

1. At the Pine Main menu, press a (for *address book*).

2. To add a single address, press a (for *add*). To create a list, press S.

3. Enter the name, nickname, and e-mail address when Pine prompts you to do so.

By entering a short nickname, you can just type the nickname when you write a message. Pine automatically retrieves the full address.

Retrieving an address from an address book

When addressing mail, you can retrieve e-mail addresses stored in an address book. In the To: or CC: of the message header, follow these steps:

1. Press Ctrl+T.

2. Press the P or N key to highlight the address you want to use.

3. Press s (for *select*) or Enter.

Storing a message in a folder

Pine provides three storage place for messages:

✦ The INBOX folder stores new messages sent to you.

✦ The saved messages folder stores copies of saved messages.

✦ The sent mail folder automatically copies and stores messages you send.

You can also create your own folders based on subject matter or name of correspondent. To create a new folder, follow these steps:

1. At the Main menu, press i (for *index*).

2. At the INBOX screen, press l (for *list folders*).

3. At the Folders List, press a (for *add*).

4. Enter the name of the new folder and press Enter.

Exiting the program

To quit Pine follow these steps:

1. At almost any place in Pine, press q (for *quit*).

Pine asks:

```
Really quit pine?
```

2. Press y or Enter to quit.

Changing options

You can customize Pine options such as printer, name and location of folders, and other things. In general, don't change these options unless you need to. Here's how to customize:

1. Type **pine**. The Main menu appears.

2. Press s (for *setup*). Pine displays four options:

• **Printer:** Chooses a printer.

• **Newpassword:** Changes your account password.

- **Config:** Modifies such things as pathnames to mail folders and address books. You can also change your name as it appears in messages.

- **Update:** Updates Pine.

3. Press p, n, c, or u to select the desired screen.

4. Use the arrows keys or press p or n to highlight the option you want to change.

5. To modify a setting, press c (for *change*) and enter a new value.

6. To return to the Pine Main menu, press m.

Getting help

To view the help screen, use the Help command at the bottom of each screen. It's usually ? or Ctrl+G, depending on the screen.

xmail

xmail is a graphical, X-based mail program.

Sending a message

1. Using the mouse, click the button in the middle of the screen labeled Send.

2. xmail creates a new window running the standard local text editor, such as emacs or vi. Type the contents of the message, save the file, and leave the editor.

xmail pops up yet another window:

3. Type the address(es) to send the message to and then press Enter.

4. Type the subject of the message.

5. Click Deliver to send the message.

If you don't want to send the message, hold down the Ctrl key while you click Deliver, and xmail discards it instead.

Reading your messages

To read your mail by using the mouse, follow these steps:

1. Run xmail if it is not already running, or double-click its icon if it is. The first new message should appear in the bottom part of the xmail window. If it doesn't, click the Newmail button to make it look for new mail.

2. If the message doesn't fit in the window, click in the gray bar to the left of the message to scroll through the body of the message.

3. If you want to delete the current message, click Delete.

4. To go to the next message, hold down the Shift key and click the Read button.

The list (or *index*) of messages with their subject lines appears in the top half of the xmail window. You can click the left and right mouse buttons in the bar to the left of the index to scroll up and down. To pick a message from the list, click the desired line in the index and then click the Read button to see the message.

Replying to a message

xmail has a convenient little Reply button that makes easy work of sending a message back to someone who wrote to you. Follow these steps:

1. Run xmail if it is not already running, or double-click its icon if it is.

2. Display the message to which you want to reply.

3. With the message on-screen, click the Reply button. If you want to include the text of the original in the reply text to edit, hold down Shift while clicking Reply.

4. Edit and send the message the same way as you would a new message. xmail provides the subject and recipient address automatically after you edit the message.

Forwarding a message

It may not be a snap to remember, but there's a simple way to send a copy of any incoming message to a third party in xmail. Here's how:

1. Run xmail if it is not already running, or double-click its icon if it is.

2. Display the message that you want to forward.

3. Hold down the Shift key while clicking the Send button.

4. Edit and send the message the same way you would a new message. xmail provides the subject after you edit the message and lets you type the recipient's address.

Reading saved messages in a mailbox

Use the following procedure to re-read messages that you previously saved in a mailbox or folder.

1. Using the mouse, move the cursor to the area in the center of the screen labeled File:.

2. Type the name of the mailbox to use.

3. Click the Folder button.

Saving a message

To save incoming mail messages for later use by storing them in a mailbox, follow these steps:

1. Display the message you want to save.

2. Using the mouse, move the cursor to the area in the center of the screen labeled File:.

3. Type the name of the mailbox you want to use.

4. Click the Save button.

Sending Mail Using Other Mail Programs

Details vary, but the steps are generally similar to those outlined for the four programs described in this part.

1. Tell the program that you want to send a message.

2. Give the address to send the message to.

3. Enter the message and subject.

4. Tell the program that you're done.

If you're using a personal computer of some sort, your incoming mail is probably stored on a central machine instead of being automatically delivered to your PC. In that case, you usually have to tell the mail program on the PC to fetch your new mail from the central machine before you can read it. The commands to do so vary considerably, unfortunately, so you'll have to get local advice.

Connecting to Other Computers

Several facilities can put you into direct contact with other computers on the Internet. This part describes some of the methods you can use.

In this part...

- ✔ Using telnet to connect to and disconnect from remote computers
- ✔ Using rlogin and rsh to log in to other computers on the Net as though you were connected to them directly
- ✔ Using anonymous FTP to connect to Internet systems
- ✔ Using FTP and rcp to copy files to and retrieve files from other computers
- ✔ Uncompressing retrieved files
- ✔ Using IRC to chat with other users on the Net

Connecting to Remote Computers by Using telnet

The `telnet` program lets you log in to and use other computers on the Net as if you were sitting in front of one of their terminals.

1. To run `telnet`, type the host name of the computer you want to log in to. On line-oriented systems, type the host name on the command line.

2. The `telnet` program connects to the remote system. In the process, it tells you the *escape character* to press if you have trouble disconnecting from the remote computer later.

3. Log in to the remote system as if you were connected directly.

After you connect, the remote system may ask you what kind of terminal you are using. If you choose the wrong terminal type, the information on your screen will be scrambled. If `telnet` makes a suggestion, accept it and see what happens. Common terminal types are VT100, ANSI, and 3101.

Disconnecting from Remote Computers by Using telnet

To end a `telnet` session, you log out and end the connection by doing the following:

1. Log out from the remote system as though you were connected to it directly. `telnet` closes the connection and, on most systems, exits.

2. If the remote system won't log you out and you're using a line-oriented system, try pressing the escape character, which is usually Ctrl+]. A prompt that says `telnet>` appears.

3. If you don't get the `telnet>` prompt in a few seconds, press Enter. The prompt should appear.

4. After the prompt appears, type **quit** and then press Enter.

5. `telnet` closes the connection and exits.

Connecting to Remote Computers by Using rlogin

rlogin provides the same function as telnet, but the advantage of rlogin is that you can automatically log in to a different system. However, rlogin is not as widely supported as telnet. If rlogin doesn't work, use telnet instead.

To connect to another system by using rlogin, do the following:

1. Type **rlogin** and the name of the computer, as in **rlogin shamu**.

2. After rlogin connects to the remote computer, everything you type is sent to the remote computer, and its responses are returned to your screen. You are usually logged in automatically.

If your user name on the other computer is different from your user name on your own computer, type it after -l:

```
rlogin shamu -l king
```

See later in this part for how to arrange for automatic login.

rlogin may ask what kind of terminal you are using. If it makes a suggestion, accept it and then see what happens. Common terminal types are VT100, ANSI, and 3101.

Disconnecting from Remote Computers by Using rlogin

To end an rlogin session, you log out by doing the following:

✦ The normal way to exit is to log out from the remote computer, usually by typing **logout** or **exit**.

✦ If the other end won't let go, press Enter, then type ~. (a tilde and a period), and press Enter again. rlogin disconnects and exits.

Running Commands on Remote Computers by Using rsh

rsh is a junior version of rlogin, which runs one command at a time on a remote system.

1. Run rsh, giving it the name of the remote system and the command to run:

```
rsh shamu who
```

(This command runs the who command on a computer named shamu.)

2. If your login name on the other system is different from the one you use on your own computer, include that login name on the command line after -l:

```
rsh shamu -l king who
```

On some UNIX systems, the name rsh runs a useless *restricted shell*. In that case, this command's name is remsh or rshell.

rsh doesn't properly run full-screen programs that take character-at-a-time user input, such as text editors like emacs or vi, or mail programs like elm or pine. To run full-screen programs, use rlogin instead.

Logging In Automatically by Using rlogin and rsh

You can arrange for the rlogin and rsh commands to log you on without asking for your name or password. If a group of computers is administered together, the group often has a shared user community, so anyone allowed to log in to one of the computers in the group can actually log in to any of the computers. To handle this case, a system file lists all the hosts whose users are "equivalent" to this one. On UNIX systems, this file is called /etc/hosts.equiv, and the file is called something similar on other machines.

For example, if machine abel has a hosts.equiv file that contains the name of machine baker, then anyone on baker can rlogin to abel by using the same user name, without giving a password.

If your system uses the NIS, which is a system that shares ID information among a group of computers, the system consults an NIS hosts.equiv database in addition to its regular file. To see the database, type

```
ypcat hosts.equiv
```

In the other situation, you have accounts on several hosts, but the accounts are not all under the same management. In that case, you arrange your own rlogin setup. Here's how:

1. On each machine, create a file called .rhosts on UNIX systems, or just rhosts on others.

2. In this file, list all the other host computers on which you have accounts. Put your user name on that system after the host name, separated by a space. For example, if your user name is sam on systems Abel and Baker and tilden on system Clarissa, your .rhosts files should contain

```
Abel sam
Baker sam
Clarissa tilden
```

Connecting to a Remote System by Using FTP

Use the following procedure to log in to a computer on the Net for purposes of copying files to or from your computer.

1. Run the FTP program, giving it the name of the system to connect to by typing **ftp ntw.org**.

2. A message confirming that you are connected appears. Then the program asks for a login name and password. If you have an account on that system, use the same name and password you use for a direct or telnet login. The screen looks like the following:

```
Connected to shamu.ntw.org.
220 FTP server (Version 4.1 8/1/91) ready.
Name: elvis
331 Password required for elvis.
Password: type password here
```

On most systems, you can create a file called .netrc (or plain Netrc on non-UNIX systems). This file contains the login name for each system you use often. Each line lists a machine, the login name, and the password for that machine, like this:

```
machine shamu.ntw.org login king password sinatra
```

When you FTP to that system, it logs you in automatically.

On some versions of FTP, you can place a default line at the end of the .netrc file to say what login name to use for systems not listed:

```
default login anonymous password elvis@ntw.org
```

Connecting by Using Anonymous FTP

Anonymous FTP lets you connect to Internet systems that provide files available to the public. On those systems, rather than logging in with your own name, you log in as anonymous and use your e-mail address, or the word *guest,* as the password.

1. Run the FTP program.

2. After the remote computer asks for your login name, enter **anonymous**.

3. After the remote computer prompts for your password, enter your e-mail address. If the system suggests *guest* as the password, type **guest** instead. The prompts appear as follows:

```
ftp internic.net
Connected to internic.net.
220 *****Welcome to the InterNIC Registration Host
     *****
Name: anonymous
331 Guest login ok, send "guest" as password.
Password: type e-mail address or guest here
230 Guest login ok, access restrictions apply.
```

Quitting FTP

To disconnect from the remote computer, type **quit.**

Listing the Files in a Directory by Using FTP

After you log in by using FTP, you need to look for the files you want to retrieve.

1. Type **dir**, short for "directory."

2. You see lots of messages, including a list of the files and subdirectories in the current directory. Following is a listing of the messages that appear:

```
ftp> dir
200 PORT command successful.
150 Opening ASCII mode data connection for /bin/ls.
total 23
drwxrwxr-x 19 root   archive  512 Jun 24 12:09 doc
drwxrwxr-x  5 root   archive  512 May 18 08:14 edu
drwxr-xr-x 31 root   wheel    512 Jul 12 10:37 systems
drwxr-xr-x  3 root   archive  512 Jun 25 1992 vendorware
. . . lots of other stuff ...
226 Transfer complete.
1341 bytes received in 0.77 seconds (1.7 Kbytes/s)
```

If the directory is so big that it doesn't fit on-screen, you can ask for just part of the directory by using wildcards. For example, dir c* asks for just the files starting with the letter *c*.

If you want to store the directory listing on your own computer, you can put the name of a local file into which to store the listing. Use the dir command, followed by a period (to indicate that you want a listing of the current directory), followed by the filename in which to store the result, like this:

```
ftp> dir . file-list
200 PORT command successful.
150 Opening ASCII mode data connection for /bin/ls.
226 Transfer complete.
45341 bytes received in 42 seconds (1.0 Kbytes/s)
```

Moving to Other Directories by Using FTP

Use the following procedure to change directories on the remote computer.

1. Type **cd** and the name of the directory to change to.

```
ftp> cd edu
250 CWD command successful.
```

2. Then use the dir command to see what's in the new directory.

On many systems, the interesting stuff is stored in a directory called pub.

Retrieving Files by Using FTP

To copy files from the remote computer to your own computer, you first need to set up to retrieve the files. Then you retrieve them by using the get command.

1. Use the cd command to move to the directory where the file(s) you want are on the remote computer.

2. If the files are not plain text, type **image** to tell FTP to transfer the files as binary images, not text files.

```
ftp> image
```

```
200 Type set to I.
```

3. Type **get**, the filename on the remote computer, and the filename to use on your computer (the local filename). If you want to use the same name, you can omit the local filename. Following is what appears on-screen:

```
ftp> get intro.txt info-file
local: info-file remote: intro.txt
200 PORT command successful.
150 Opening ASCII mode data connection for intro.txt
    (5243 bytes).
226 Transfer complete.
5359 bytes received in 0 seconds (5.2 Kbytes/s)
```

4. FTP retrieves the file and displays a message about it.

FTP can take a long time to retrieve a large file. For a file retrieved from a distant site, allow one second for every 1,000 characters in the file.

If you retrieve a nontext file and it arrives smashed and unusable, 95 percent of the time you forgot to type **image** before you retrieved it.

Retrieving Groups of Files by Using FTP

To copy a group of files with one mget command, you do the following:

1. Move to the directory that contains the files and, if appropriate, set image mode, as described in the preceding section.

2. Type **mget** (for *multiple get*) followed by the names of the files to get. You can also use patterns, notably *, which means all files in the directory.

3. mget asks you about each file that matches the names and patterns in the list. Press y to transfer the file or n to skip it.

Use the prompt command to turn off the prompting for each file so that it will transfer all the files in the group without asking.

Downloading Retrieved Files to Your PC by Using FTP

If you are using a local PC to dial into an Internet host, FTP retrieves files to the Internet host, not to your local PC. After the files are on your Internet host, you have to download them to your PC.

Downloading details vary, but (generally speaking) you do the following:

1. Type the command to the host to start the downloading program, such as **sz** for Zmodem or **kermit** for Kermit, and the names of the files to download.

2. If your PC terminal program doesn't start downloading automatically, you need to tell it to start downloading, typically by using an Alt+key combination. If you don't know the appropriate key combination, refer to your terminal program's manual.

3. After the files are downloaded, delete the copies on the Internet host so that you aren't charged for the disk space.

The Terminal program that comes with Microsoft Windows 3.1 can transfer binary files by using either Xmodem or Kermit. To choose a protocol, use the `Settings Binary Transfers` command. To begin a file transfer, use the `Transfers Receive Binary File` command.

Sending Files to Remote Systems by Using FTP

If the permissions allow, you can send files to a remote system.

1. Move to the directory in which you want to store the file on the remote computer.

2. If the files contain binary data, set image mode, as previously described in the section on "Retrieving Files by Using FTP."

3. Type **put**, the filename on your computer (the local filename), and the filename to use on the remote system. You can omit the remote filename if it's the same as the local filename. The following appears on-screen:

```
ftp> put nigel nigel data
local: myfile remote: stored-file
200 PORT command successful.
150 Opening ASCII mode data connection for nigel-data.
226 Transfer complete.
795 bytes sent in 0 seconds (0.78 Kbytes/s)
```

You can copy a group of files to the remote computer by using the `mput` command. In step 3, type **mput** and the name of the files to store, or a pattern that matches the name of the files to store. The pattern * means all files in the local directory.

As it copies the files, `mput` asks you about each file. Press y to store a file or n to skip it.

If you want to store a group of files without FTPasking you about each one, type **prompt** to turn off name prompting.

Summary of FTP Commands

Here's a short list of useful FTP commands, including a few not otherwise mentioned:

Command	Description
get old new	Copy remote file *old* to local file *new.* You can omit *new* if same name as *old.*
put old new	Copy local file *old* to remote file *new.* You can omit *new* if same name as *old.*
del xyz	Delete file *xyz* on a remote system.
cd newdir	Change to directory newdir on the remote machine.
cdup	Change to the next higher directory (the parent directory).
lcd newdir	Change to the directory newdir on the local machine.
asc	Transfer files in ASCII mode (use for text files).
bin	Transfer files in binary or image mode (all other files).
quit	Leave FTP.
dir pat	List files whose names match the pattern *pat.* If you omit *pat,* list all files.
mget pat	Get files whose names match the pattern *pat.*
mput pat	Put files whose names match the pattern *pat.*
mdel pat	Delete remote files whose names match the pattern *pat.*

Copying Files from Remote Computers by Using rcp

A somewhat easier way to transfer files on systems that support it is by using the rcp command. The rcp command is available on the same computers (mainly UNIX systems) that support rlogin and rsh.

1. Type **rcp**, the remote filename, and the local filename. To copy a file named mydata from the host named pumpkin to the local machine and give that file the new name of pumpkindata, type **rcp pumpkin:mydata pumpkindata**.

2. rcp doesn't say a thing if the file transfers successfully, but you do see a message if there is a problem.

To use the rcp command, the remote system must be set up so it can automatically log you in to do the copy. For more information, *see* the discussion on rlogin in Part IV.

In rcp, you refer to a file on another system with the system's host name, a colon, and the filename, such as othersys:myfile. If the file is in another directory, use the usual slash separator, such as **othersys:dirname/myfile**.

To copy a file if your user name is different on the other system, you just type your user name and @ before the host name, like this:

```
rcp steph@pumpkin:mydata pumpkindata
```

To copy to or from another user's directory on the remote computer (if the permissions allow you to do so), use a tilde (~) and the user name as the directory name:

```
rcp pumpkin:~tracy/somefile tracyfile
```

rcp is extremely taciturn, saying nothing at all unless something goes wrong. If you are copying a great deal of files over a network, it can take a while (like a couple of minutes), so you may have to be more patient than usual while waiting for it to do its work.

Copying Files by Using rcp

To upload a file to a remote computer that supports rcp, do the following:

1. Type **rcp**, the local filename, and the remote filename. To copy a file named pumpkindata from the local computer to the host named pumpkin and to rename that file as mydata, type **rcp pumpkindata pumpkin:mydata**.

2. Remember, rcp doesn't say a thing if the file transfers successfully. If there is a problem, you see a message.

Copying All the Files in a Directory by Using rcp

1. To copy all the files from the current directory on the remote computer to the current directory on your computer, type **rcp**, the remote directory name, a period (which stands for the current directory), and the -r (for *recursive*) flag. For example, if you type **rcp pumpkin:projectdir**, you're copying the directory projectdir on host pumpkin into the current directory (indicated by a period) on the local machine.

2. To copy all the files from the current directory on your local computer to the current directory on the remote computer, type **rcp**, a period (which stands for the current directory), the remote directory name, and the -r (for *recursive*) flag.

Uncompressing Files You Have Retrieved

Files on anonymous FTP systems are usually stored in one of several forms that save space and make them easier to transfer, but you still need to decode them.

The filename extension (the part after the dot) tells you how the file is coded and, more importantly, which program you need to use to decode the file. Many compression and uncompression programs can be FTPed from wuarchive.wustl.edu in the directory /packages/compression.

Following is a table of common file types:

Type	Description
Text	Plain text that can be printed, displayed, and edited with the usual printing and text editing programs.
Compressed	A coded form, with many variants, that saves space.
Archived	Many files combined into one (most archived files are also compressed).
Images	Digitized pictures in GIF, JPEG, or other image format.
Uuencoded	Special format that disguises a nontext file as text so it can be e-mailed.
Z	Z files (capital Z) are compressed files created by the UNIX compress program and are decoded with uncompress.
gz	gz and z files are created by the GNU gzip program and uncompressed by GNU gunzip. These programs are available at ftp.uu.net, prep.ai.mit.edu and other places. GNU gunzip knows about a great deal of compression formats and can decode most compressed formats that aren't also archive formats.
tar	tar (Tape ARchive) is a UNIX archiving program. To unpack a tar file on a UNIX system, type **tar xvf blurfle.tar** tar files are commonly compressed with names like blurfle.tar.Z. Uncompress them and then untar them. On some systems, tar files are called .taz files.
cpio	cpio (CoPy In and Out) is another UNIX program with its own format. To decode it on a UNIX system, type **cpio -itcv < blurfle.cpio**. Compressed cpio is also common. Uncompress the file and then uncpio it.
zip	zip files are the most common kind of compressed archives used on DOS and Windows systems. You extract files from them by using the freely available unzip command: **unzip blurfle.zip**.

Chatting with Others on the Net

Internet Relay Chat (IRC) lets people across the Internet talk to one another live. Jarkko Oikarinen at the University of Oulu Computing Center, Finland, originally wrote IRC.

The IRC consists of many channels, or *chat areas,* where a group of people can discuss a particular subject. You can also have private conversations with one person. Each user has a nickname, which is either a made-up name or your login name.

There are three channel types, each with increasing levels of privacy:

✦ **Public:** Public channels are available to all users.

✦ **Secret:** Users can tell that you are using IRC but can't see the name of the channel.

✦ **Hidden:** Other users can't see you or the channel.

Starting IRC

To start IRC, type **irc.**

To start IRC and give yourself a nickname, type **irc BadBob** (or whatever name you want to use). Two people cannot have the same nickname. If you select a nickname that is already in use, the system prompts you for a different nickname.

To start IRC and go to a particular channel, specify both a channel to enter and a nickname as follows: **irc "#cars" BadBob.** (You need to quote the # sign.)

If you don't specify a channel when you start IRC, some information about the current IRC activity is displayed:

```
+/HELP NEWUSER
*** This server was created Nov 22 1992 at 19:02:56 EST
*** There are 1003 users and 377 invisible on 146
    servers
*** 74 users have connection to the twilight zone
*** There are 374 channels.
*** I have 1 clients and 1 servers
```

You can now find out which channels are available and then join one.

Finding IRC Channels

To find out which IRC channels are available, type **/list**.

This command displays available channels, the number of users on each channel, and the subject matter of each channel. Secret and hidden channels do not appear.

Because there are many channels, the list that is shown may be quite long. You can shorten the list by typing the command **/list -MIN** *numusers*. This list shows only channels with at least *numusers* users.

You can also use wildcards. To see all channels that start with the letter *D,* for example, type

```
/list #d*
```

Joining an IRC Channel

All channel names have a # before them.

To join a channel, type **/join #channel**. For example, to join the channel called #cars, you type

```
/join #cars
```

Quitting IRC

Use any of the following commands to quit IRC: /BYE, /EXIT, /QUIT, or /SIGNOFF.

Getting Help with IRC Commands

If you need help with IRC commands, type **/help.** Help displays a list of available commands.

If you know the name of the command you want to use, but can't remember what it does, type **/help commandname.**

Help displays information about the specified command.

To quit the Help mode, press Enter. Sometimes you have to press the Enter key several times.

Many advanced IRC commands exist but are not described in this section. You can create automated scripts to connect to IRC and even start up your own channel. If you want more information about IRC, a good place to look is the newsgroup alt.irc. *See* Part VIII for details about reading newsgroups.

Chatting by Using IRC Commands

To *chat* with others, simply enter text and press Enter to send it to someone.

✦ A message that you send to everyone is displayed with a preceding >, and your nickname is displayed in angle brackets, as shown: `<BadBob> >Hello`.

✦ A message that you send privately to one person is displayed with a preceding ->, and the nickname of the person you sent it to is displayed in asterisks. For example, if you send a private message "Yikes!" to Eskimo Joe, it looks like this: `->*Eskimo Joe* Yikes!`

Here are a few editing commands you can use:

Command	Description
Ctrl+A	Moves the cursor to the beginning of the line.
Ctrl+B	Moves the cursor back a character.
Ctrl+D	Deletes the character under the cursor.
Ctrl+E	Goes to the end of the line.
Ctrl+F	Moves the cursor forward a character.
Ctrl+K	Deletes (kills) from the cursor to the end of the line.

Summary of IRC Commands

Commands are preceded by /. Press Enter after you type the command.

Command	Description
/away message	Tells other users that you will be away from your computer for a while. When you get back, type **/away** again to rejoin the conversation.
/channel #	Joins the specified channel. The name of the channel must be a number. This command is the same as /join.
/clear	Clears the screen if it becomes cluttered.
/invite name #	Lets you invite a user who is currently on IRC to join your channel.
/join #	Joins the specified channel. The name of the channel must be a number. This command is the same as /channel.
/list	Displays a list of available channels, the topics of the channels, and the number of users on the channels. This command does not work for hidden or secret channels.

(continued)

Command	Description
/msg name message	Sends a private message to the specified user. Other users cannot see this message.
/nick newnickname	Changes your nickname to the new one you enter.
/query name	Asks someone to have a private conversation.
/summon name	Lets you summon a user who is not using IRC to enter the channel. You must enter the full login address of the user (such as joe@computer.com).
/users	Displays a list of the users logged into the system.
/who channelname	Lists all the users on the channel you specify.
/whois name	Displays the login name and host computer name of the specified user.

Having an IRC Private Conversation

If you have a private conversation with another user, only the two of you can see anything typed. The other person does not have to be on the same channel as you but does have to be using IRC.

To ask another user to enter into a private conversation, type **/query** *name,* where *name* is the nickname of the other user. If the other user repeats the command by using your nickname, you establish a private dialogue.

To leave private mode, type **/query.**

Finding Resources on the Net

So many resources are available on the Internet that finding them can be harder than using them. This part describes programs that you can use to search for and retrieve information on the Net.

Your local computer system may have one or all of these programs. Trying typing the name of the search tool (**gopher**, **WAIS**, or whatever) to see whether your system has it installed. If not, you can always telnet to a computer that does have these programs available.

In this part...

✔ Using Archie and Xarchie to find where files are stored

✔ Using Gopher and Xgopher to find files on the Net

✔ Using WAIS to search for text within files

✔ Using Lynx and Mosaic to access the World Wide Web

Archie

Archie uses a text pattern that you enter to search for files. You need to know the name of the file you're looking for, and Archie finds sites that have the file.

There are several ways to use Archie, all of which require that you contact an Archie server:

+ Command line `Archie` program

+ Windowed `xarchie` program

+ Telnet to an Archie server

+ E-mail to an Archie server

Finding an Archie program

You system may or may not have Archie installed. If it doesn't, you can telnet to one of the sites listed in the following tables:

U.S. Public Archie Server	Location
archie.sura.net	Maryland
archie.unl.edu	Nebraska
archie.internic.net	New Jersey
archie.ans.net	New York

International Public Archie Server	Location
archie.au	Australia
archie.univie.ac.at	Austria
archie.uqam.ca	Canada
archie.funet.fi	Finland
archie.th-darmstadt.de	Germany
archie.ac.il	Israel
archie.unipi.it	Italy
archie.kuis.kyoto-u.ac.jp	Japan
archie.hana.nm.kr	Korea
archie.nz	New Zealand
archie.inesc.pt	Portugal

International Public Archie Server	Location
archie.rediris.es	Spain
archie.luth.se	Sweden
archie.switch.ch	Switzerland
archie.ncu.edu.tw	Taiwan
archie.doc.ic.ac.uk	United Kingdom

Using the Archie program

If your system has an `archie` program, you can make Archie queries directly.

1. Type **archie** and the string to search for. For example:

```
archie prune
```

Archie returns a list of the matching hosts and names.

2. Use anonymous FTP (described in Part VI) to retrieve the files.

Archie usually returns more answers than can fit on a single screen. To view the list one page at a time, use the | character and the `more` command:

```
archie garlic | more
```

To save the list in a file, use the > character to redirect the list like this:

```
archie garlic > garlicfiles
```

You can use the command line options in the following table to control how the `archie` program works.

Archie Modifier	Equivalent Telnet Command	Meaning
-c	subcase	Sets search mode for a case-sensitive substring.
-e	exact	Sets search mode for an exact string match (the default).
-r	regex	Sets search mode for a regular expression search.
-s	sub	Sets search mode for a substring search.
-l		Lists one match per line.
-t	sortby	Sorts the output by date, newest first.

(continued)

Archie Modifier	Equivalent Telnet Command	Meaning
-m#	maxhits	Sets the maximum number of matches to return (the default 95).
-h *host*		Specifies the Archie server to use.
-L		Lists the known Archie servers and the current default.

Connecting to Archie by using telnet

If you don't have a local `archie` program, you can telnet to a site that has Archie. Here's how:

1. Telnet to the nearest Archie site, listed in the "Finding an Archie program" section. *See* Part VI for how to use the `telnet` command.

2. Log in as **archie** (do not try to log in as yourself). The `archie>` prompt is displayed.

3. If you don't want to use the standard sub search (described in the preceding section), type **set search xxx**, where *xxx* is the type of search you want (**subcase**, **exact**, or **regex**).

4. Type **prog** followed by the string to search for. Archie returns a list of the matching files.

5. To get a description of a name or term, type **whatis** and the name or term.

6. After making as many searches as you want, type **exit** to leave the `archie` program.

7. Use anonymous FTP (described in Part VI) to retrieve the files.

Requesting information from Archie

archie has four different search modes. How much you know about the name of the files you are looking for will determine the search method you should use. See the following table for details.

Search Method	Meaning
sub	Matches the search string anywhere in the filename, disregarding capitalization.
subcase	Matches the search string exactly as given anywhere in the filename, including matching capitalization.
exact	Searches for this exact filename, including matching capitalization. Use this option if possible, since it's the fastest.
regex	Uses UNIX "regular expressions" to define the pattern for Archie's search. See the next table for more information.

Special Character in Archie Regular Expression	Meaning
*	Matches any number of whatever it follows.
[ ]	Match any one of the characters in brackets.
^	Matches the beginning of the name. Inside square brackets, it means to match any character except the ones in brackets.
$	Matches the end of the name.

For example, ^[0-9]$ matches a name consisting entirely of digits, and tr.ck matches *trick, track, truck,* or *trzck.*

Sending e-mail to Archie

You can submit Archie queries by e-mail.

Send an e-mail message to archie@*server,* where *server* is any of the Archie servers listed earlier in this part.

The contents of the message are commands in nearly the same form you give to telnet Archie. See the following table of commands.

Archie then mails back its response.

Command	Description
prog	Searches assuming a regular expression search (regex).
whatis	Supplies the keyword for the software description database search.
compress	Sends the reply in a compressed and uuencoded format.
servers	Returns a list of Archie servers.
path	Gives the e-mail address you want Archie to use to respond to your mail request in case the return address in your mail isn't correct.
help	Returns the help text for e-mail Archie.
quit	Ends the request to Archie.

For example, the following command searches for files whose filenames start with *font* and end with *.txt:*

```
prog font.*txt
```

Archie servers are so heavily loaded that a telnet, command line, or window Archie command can take several minutes to run. In that case, you might consider e-mailing your request so that you don't have to wait. For large queries, a 400-line e-mail message is easier to handle than a 400-line telnet or windowed response.

Gopher

The Gopher program is an easy-to-use, menu-driven search tool. You can use the menus to find files on systems all over the world, including information that comes from Archie, telnet, and FTP.

Your system may or may not have Gopher installed. If it doesn't, you can telnet to one of the sites listed in the following tables.

U.S. Public Gopher Server	Location	Login (If Not gopher)
infopath.ucsd.edu	California	infopath
grits.valdosta.peachnet.edu	Georgia	
gopher.netsys.com	Illinois	enews
panda.uiowa.edu	Iowa	
inform.umd.edu	Maryland	
gopher.ora.com	Massachusetts	
wsuaix.csc.wsu.edu	Michigan	wsuinfo
consultant.micro.umn.edu	Minnesota	
gopher.msu.edu	Mississippi	
nicol.jvnc.net	New Jersey	NICOL
sunsite.unc.edu	North Carolina	
cat.ohiolink.edu	Ohio	
envirolink.hss.cmu.edu	Pennsylvania	envirolink
gopher.virginia.edu	Virginia	gwis
telnet.wiscinfo.wisc.edu	Wisconsin	wiscinfo
info.anu.edu.au	Australia	info
finfo.tu-graz.ac.at	Austria	info
nstn.ns.ca	Canada	fred
tolten.puc.cl	Chile	
gopher.denet.dk	Denmark	
ecnet.ec	Ecuador	
gopher.th-darmstadt.de	Germany	

U.S. Public Gopher Server	Location	Login (If Not gopher)
gopher.isnet.is	Iceland	
siam.mi.cnr.it	Italy	
gopher.torun.edu.pl	Poland	
gopher.uv.es	Spain	
info.sunet.se	Sweden	
gopher.brad.ac.uk	United Kingdom	info

Using Gopher's menus

You can use Gopher menus to find files on systems all over the world, including information that comes from Archie, telnet, FTP, and so on.

All Gopher programs have one feature in common — they show you a series of menus. Menus can contain these types of items:

+ Menu items that refer to other menus

+ File items that refer to files of text, images, or other data

+ Search items that let you type some search text and create a custom menu of items found in the search

+ Telnet items, which start an interactive telnet session to a host that provides a particular service; if you need to login to the host, Gopher tells you the login name to use

The contents of each menu are determined by the remote Gopher server, not your Gopher client program, so no matter which program you use, you can get to the same material. Some Gopher client programs have limits on the kinds of files they can handle; in particular, the UNIX Gopher program can display only files that contain plain text, although it can copy any file to your local machine.

Starting Gopher

Running gopher on a UNIX system lets you see Gopher information.

1. If your system has the gopher program, skip to the next step. Otherwise, use the telnet program to log in to a UNIX system that does, and skip to step 3. (*See* Part VI for how to telnet.)

2. Run the program by typing **gopher**.

3. You see a menu like this:

```
Internet Gopher Information Client v1.1Root gopher
server:gopher.micro.umn.edu
-> 1.  Information About Gopher/
   2.  Computer Information/
```

```
 3.   Discussion Groups/
 4.   Fun & Games/
 5.   Internet file server (ftp) sites/
 6.   Libraries/
 7.   News/
 8.   Other Gopher and Information Servers/
 9.   Phone Books/
10.   Search Gopher Titles at the University of Minnesota <?>
11.    Search lots of places at the University of Minnesota <?>
12. University of Minnesota Campus Information/
Press ? for Help, q to Quit, u to go up a menu
Page: 1/1
```

4. To move to a particular item, use the up and down arrow keys or type the line number of the item. Items that end with a slash display other menus; items that end with something in < > are search or telnet items (discussed later in this part); and items that end with neither are files.

5. To select an item, move to it and press Enter.

6. To leave Gopher, press q. If it asks whether you really want to quit, press y.

If the menu is larger than the screen, press + and - or use the cursor keys to scroll up and down. To return to the preceding menu, press u. To return to the first menu, press m.

Searching for information by using Gopher

You can tell Gopher to search its database based on text you enter. If you can't find the information you are looking for by moving around the menus (as described in the preceding section), try searching. In Gopher menus, menu items that can be searched are indicated by <?>.

1. Run Gopher as described in the preceding section.

2. Select a search item by moving to it and pressing Enter.

3. Gopher pops up a box in which you can type search terms. Type a word or words that describe what you are looking for, and press Enter. Gopher shows you a menu consisting of the items that matched.

4. Select items on that menu as you would on any other menu.

Gopher has special *CSO* searches for looking up people in organization phone books. They work nearly the same way as regular searches, except that you can enter a lot of different facts about the person you're looking for. Usually, however, you just need to type the person's first and last name and press Enter.

Saving files that Gopher finds

You can copy files that you find with Gopher to your own computer. You can save files only if you are using a Gopher client program on your own computer. If you are telnetting to a Gopher server, you have to mail them to yourself.

1. Gopher shows text files one screen at a time. Press the spacebar to move from screen to screen or q to stop viewing the file.

2. Press s to save the file on your own computer, or press m to send the file to yourself as e-mail. Gopher asks for your e-mail address. (*See* Part II for information about e-mail.)

If you dial in to a gopher program from a PC by using a terminal program such as Kermit, Crosstalk, or ProComm, you can download files directly to your system. Follow these steps:

1. On the menu on which the file appears, move to the file item but do not press Enter.

2. Press D (for *download*).

3. Gopher pops up a window listing the download schemes it can use, with numbers by each one. Type the number of one that your terminal program supports, most often Kermit, Zmodem, or Xmodem.

4. If it doesn't do so automatically, tell your modem program to start downloading. The information is copied to your disk.

Using Gopher to telnet

If you find something interesting in Gopher, and Gopher says that you have to telnet to another system to see it, Gopher offers to do the telnetting for you automatically. On Gopher menus, telnet items end with <TEL>. (*See* Part VI for information about telnet.)

1. Select a telnet item by moving the cursor to it and pressing Enter. Gopher pops up a window warning you that you are about to telnet to someplace else and giving you the login name to use.

2. The telnet session starts. Log in when prompted to, using the name supplied.

3. Use the system to find the information you want.

4. Log out. You return to Gopher.

Any system that Gopher can telnet to, you can also telnet to yourself. If you find a system useful, make a note of the name of the system and the login name, and telnet there directly next time.

Using bookmarks

You can tell Gopher to place "bookmarks" at particular menus and items for later reference.

✦ To put a bookmark on the current menu, press A. (Yes, that's a capital A.)

✦ To see a menu of all your bookmarks, press v.

✦ To select an item from that menu, move the cursor to it and press Enter.

✦ To delete an item from the bookmark menu, move the cursor to it and press d.

If you telnet to Gopher, bookmarks are remembered only until you log out. If you run Gopher on your local computer, bookmarks are remembered in a file and are available at any time.

Command summary

Gopher Basic Command	Description
Enter	Selects current item, same as cursor right.
u	Goes back to the preceding menu (same as cursor left).
+	Moves to the next menu page.
−	Moves to the preceding menu page.
m	Goes to the main menu.
digits	Goes to particular menu item (terminate with Enter).
/	Searches the menu for a string.
n	Searches for the next match.
q	Leaves Gopher.
=	Describes the current item.

Gopher Bookmark Command	Description
a	Adds the current item to the bookmark list.
A	Adds the current menu to the list.
v	Views bookmarks as a menu.
d	Deletes the current bookmark.

Gopher File Command	Description
m	Mails the current file to a user.
s	Saves the current file (not for telnet).
p	Prints the current file (not for telnet).
D	Downloads the current file.

Lynx

The `Lynx` program lets you "surf" the World Wide Web, which is a hypertext system that links together many kinds of information all over the world. By displaying a Web document (or "page") and selecting a highlighted topic on the page, you can move from page to page to find information. The Web cannot access as much information as Gopher and WAIS, but the information it has is usefully linked together.

Depending on the local Lynx configuration, links may be highlighted in bold or reverse video, or with a code number in brackets after the item. In the following examples, each link is displayed in bold. You can follow these links to see other information.

1. Type **lynx**. The Lynx startup screen is displayed, containing several links to other resources.

2. Move the cursor to the desired link with the up and down arrow keys, and then press Enter. (Use the up and down arrow keys even if the links are on the same line.) On a system that displays links as numbers in brackets, you can also type the number of the link you want and then press Enter.

If the page doesn't fit on-screen, press the spacebar or + to go forward or B to go back.

Web pages can display pictures. However, Lynx is a text-only program and cannot display pictures. Instead, it puts a note saying [INLINE] where each picture would have gone.

Going directly to a page

If you know the name of a Web page, you can go directly to that page:

1. In Lynx, press G (as in *go*).

2. Type the name of the Web page and press Enter. A typical Web address might look like this:

```
http://www.dummies.com/
```

Going back to a previous page

There are two ways to view previous pages:

✦ To move to the last page you viewed, press the left arrow key.

✦ Lynx keeps a list of Web pages you have viewed in the past. An easy way of going to previously viewed pages is by using this "History list."

1. Press the Backspace key (some versions of Lynx say to use Delete, but they mean Backspace) or Ctrl+H. The History list appears.

2. Depending on your system, use the arrow keys to select the page you want or press the number next to the desired page.

3. Press Enter. Lynx displays the selected page.

Searching the World Wide Web

1. In Lynx, type a slash (/).

2. Enter the search words that you want Lynx to use to find Web sites. Separate words with spaces.

3. Press Enter. Lynx displays a list of the pages it finds. You can now select a page to view.

Command summary

Command	Description
up arrow	Goes to the preceding screen.
down arrow	Goes to the next screen.
left arrow	Goes to the preceding link or page.
right arrow	Goes to the next link or page.
Enter	Goes to the next link or page.
(number)	Enters the number next to a link to go to that link or page.
space	Goes to the next screen.
/	Searches for Web pages.
Backspace or Ctrl+H	Views the History list.
g	Goes directly to a page.
h	Views the Help screen.
m	Goes to the main screen (the starting screen).

Command	Description
o	Changes Lynx options.
p	Prints the current page.
q	Quits Lynx.

The keys used to enter commands may differ depending on your system and keyboard. If some commands don't seem to work properly, press O (as in *options*). Doing so displays an option screen that lets you change the keys you use to enter some commands.

Netscape and Mosaic

Netscape and Mosaic are graphical, Motif-based Web browsers. Because they run in a graphical environment, they can display pictures as well as text. Both browsers let you "surf the Web," moving from document (or page) to document by clicking hyperlinks.

Note: The several different versions of Mosiac all work basically the same way. NCSA Mosaic is described here.

Starting up

To start Mosaic, type **mosaic**. To start Netscape, type **netscape**.The *home page,* or starting point, appears.

At the top or bottom of the screen (depending on the version of the program) are several buttons you can click to move around the Web. You can also access the functions that these buttons provide by using the drop-down menu.

Going to a new page

There are two ways to move from Web page to Web page:

✦ Click a hyperlink. *Hyperlinks* are words on a page that are either underlined or displayed in a different color than the rest of the text. Sometimes, you can click a picture to go to another page.

✦ Type the name of the Web site as described in the following steps.

If you know the name of a Web site, you can go directly to that page.

1. Choose File⇨Open URL in Mosaic, or choose File⇨Open Location in Netscape.

2. Type the name of the Web site and press Enter.

URL stands for *Uniform Resource Locator,* which is the type of address used on the Web. A typical URL might look like this:

```
http://www.dummies.com/
```

In Netscape, you can also click the cursor in the Location: field on-screen and type the URL there.

Going back to a previous page

There are two ways to view a page you've already looked at:

✦ To move to the last page you viewed, click the Back button at the top or bottom of the screen.

✦ Netscape and Mosaic keep a list of Web pages that you have viewed in the past. An easy way of going to previously viewed pages is by using this list, or *History.*

In Mosaic:

1. Choose Navigate⇨Window History. The Window History window appears. This window lists the pages you have viewed.

2. Double-click the name of the page you want to view. It is displayed again.

3. Click Dismiss to make the History window go away.

In Netscape:

1. Choose <u>G</u>o. The History appears as menu items.

2. Select the desired item.

Finding places to go in Mosaic

The Navigate and Help menus contain links to interesting Web sites.

On the Navigate menu:

✦ `Internet Starting Points` lists some home pages, services, hyperlinks to other types of servers, and information for new users.

✦ `Internet Resources Meta-Index` lists various resource directories available on the Web.

On the Help menu, `What's New Page` lists new Web sites.

The Navigate menu contains an option called the *Hotlist.* The Hotlist lets you create a personal list of Web sites that you find interesting or use often.

Finding places to go in Netscape

The Directory menu contains links to interesting Web sites, including

✦ Internet Directory links to Yahoo, an excellent directory of Web sites

✦ Internet Search links to pages that let you search for Web pages by keywords

✦ What's New and What's Cool are lists of interesting pages compiled by the Netscape staff

Printing a page

1. On the File menu, choose Print. The Print window appears.

2. Enter the desired print command if it differs from the default. For example, you may want to print to a different printer than the one listed.

3. In Mosaic, select one of the four print options: plain text (without formatting); formatted text (the page will contain the fonts shown on-screen); PostScript; or HTML (prints the text and the special codes used to create the page). Netscape also offers a variety of printing options, but the defaults are usually adequate.

4. Click Print to print the document.

Saving a file

1. On the File menu, choose Save As. The Save Document window appears.

2. Select the directory in which you want to save the file.

3. Type a name for the file.

4. Select one of the four save options: plain text (without format-ting); formatted text (the page will contain the fonts shown on-screen); PostScript; or HTML (saves the text and the special codes used to create the page).

5. Click Save to save the page to a file.

You can also save text from a page by copying and pasting. To copy text, press the left mouse button and drag it over the text you want. On some systems, you click the right mouse button to indicate the end of the range of text you are copying.

Freeing disk space

The Web page History list is not cleared when you leave Mosaic, so it gets larger and will eventually consume a lot of disk space. As a result, you should occasionally clear the History list.

In Mosaic:

1. On the Navigate menu, choose Clear Global History.

2. When Mosaic prompts, confirm that you want to clear the History file.

In Netscape:

1. Choose Options⇨Network.

2. Select the Cache tab in the window that appears.

3. Click Clear Disk Cache Now.

4. Click OK to confirm that you want to clear the History.

Quitting Mosaic or Netscape

To leave Mosaic or Netscape, click the File menu and choose Exit. Click OK in the window that appears to confirm that you want to exit.

Other Resource Indexes

The Usenet archive at `rtfm.mit.edu` has useful information and references to archives elsewhere on the Net. It is indexed by the names of Usenet groups. There are two easy ways to get to it:

✦ FTP to `rtfm.mit.edu`, change the directory to `usenet-by-groups`, and then go to the newsgroup you are interested in — for example, `sci.med` for information about medicine.

✦ Send an e-mail message to `mail-server@rtfm.mit.edu` consisting of the single word *help* to get started.

Veronica

Veronica is a search tool available on some Gopher menus. It allows you to enter search words that it uses to find the topics you're looking for.

1. Select a Gopher menu item that lets you use Veronica, and press Enter. Typically, you can find one under `Other Gopher and Information Servers/`.

2. Veronica displays a menu containing a search list. Select a search option and press Enter.

Veronica prompts you as follows:

```
Enter words to search for
```

3. Type your search words in the highlighted field and then press Enter. Veronica displays a list of Gopher menus it has found.

4. When you are finished using Veronica, press Q to quit.

Veronica servers tend to be very overloaded and often return a one-line response telling you to try again later. In that case, using a different server in a different time zone may work better.

Entering search words

Veronica lets you enter wildcards and special words that help make your search more specific. This feature lets you retrieve information more quickly.

Search Option	Description
dog*	Searches for information beginning with the letters *dog*.
dogs and cats	*and* specifies that both topics must be present to be retrieved.
dogs or cats	*or* specifies that either topic will be retrieved.
dogs not cats	*not* retrieves information about dogs, but not if it also contains information about cats.

Some organizations set up a local equivalent of Veronica called *Jughead.* Jughead can search only on computers in a limited area, such as a university. While its range is far smaller than Veronica's, it is much quicker because it has a smaller search area.

WAIS

Wide Area Information Service (WAIS) is a full-text search service. That is, you give it a list of words, and it looks through a database containing a large number of documents and finds the ones that best match the search words. Unlike archie and Veronica, WAIS looks at the *contents* of files, not just at their titles.

Some versions of WAIS also have "relevance feedback." After WAIS does a search, you can mark a few of the documents that it finds as the most relevant and redo the search, in which case WAIS tries to find documents similar to the ones you mark.

If your local computer system has a WAIS program, use it. Otherwise, you can telnet to a computer that does or use WAIS via the World Wide Web (described later in this section).

1. If your computer system has a WAIS program, run it by typing **WAIS.**

If not, telnet to a computer that has WAIS. We recommend telnetting to WAIS.com, the home of WAIS. Log in as **WAIS.** After a startup delay, a directory of servers (also known as *sources*) appears.

2. Use WAIS to search for information, as described in the next few sections.

3. When you are done, press Q to quit. Depending on where you are, you may have to press it three or four times to exit.

Selecting databases to search

WAIS can search hundreds of different databases (also known as *document sources*). To tell WAIS which databases to look in while doing your search:

1. Run WAIS as described in the preceding section. You see a list of hundreds of document sources that WAIS is prepared to search.

2. When you see a document source that you think might contain the information you want, select it by pressing the spacebar or a period. You can select as many document sources as you wish.

3. Use the down arrow key or j (lowercase) to move down the list, and up arrow key or k (lowercase) to move up the list.

To move a page at a time, use J and K. When you get to the end of the list, WAIS shows you the beginning again. When you move up to the beginning, WAIS shows you the end (it's an endless loop). You can also move right to a document source on the list by pressing / (slash) followed by the name of the document source.

Now you are ready to tell WAIS what to search for.

If you can't find any document sources, select the document source called *Database of Servers* and search through it for more possible databases. Follow these steps to do so:

1. Type **WAIS**.

2. Select the Database of Servers by moving to it and pressing the spacebar or . (period).

3. Press W to tell WAIS that you want to enter the text to search for.

4. Enter some words describing the kinds of topics you want. Separate each word with a space.

5. Press Enter to search for document sources. You are asked whether you want to add additional search words. When you are ready, press Enter to start the search.

6. A list of document sources is displayed. Select one by using the arrow keys or typing the line number. Then press Enter.

7. Press the spacebar to look at the source description (the description of the document that it finds). If it is more than one page, press the spacebar to page through it. To add the server to the list that WAIS can use, press u.

8. Repeat these steps for as many sources as you want.

9. Press s to return to the WAIS sources screen.

Searching for text within documents

When you tell WAIS what words or phrases to search for, be sure that you already selected the document sources to search in.

1. After you select the WAIS document sources you want, press Enter to prepare to search.

2. The current list of keywords appears. You can press Ctrl+U to clear it if needed, and then you can add new terms if desired. Press Enter again to perform the search. After the search is complete, WAIS displays a list of documents, as shown in the following figure:

```
SWAIS                                  Search Results                         Items: 40
 #    Score     Source                        Title                            Lines
001:  [1000] (cmns-moon.think)  SUMMER PUDDING(D)           USENET Cookbook       55
002:  [1000] (         recipes)  Anne Louie Re: BREAD: Bread Recipes Coll      1101
003:  [ 826] (cmns-moon.think)  XMAS-PUDDING(D)             USENET Cookbook      107
004:  [ 780] (cmns-moon.think)  VIGILIA-1(M)                USENET Cookbook      118
005:  [ 570] (cmns-moon.think)  YOGURT-FROZ-1(D)            USENET Cookbook       56
006:  [ 559] (cmns-moon.think)  FRUIT-TART(D)               USENET Cookbook       51
007:  [ 547] (cmns-moon.think)  FRUIT-CAKE-1(C)             USENET Cookbook      104
008:  [ 547] (cmns-moon.think)  CURRIED-FRUIT(D)            USENET Cookbook       59
009:  [ 535] (cmns-moon.think)  FRUIT-SOUP(SPU)             USENET Cookbook      118
010:  [ 524] (cmns-moon.think)  FRUIT-SALAD(D)              USENET Cookbook       97
011:  [ 524] (cmns-moon.think)  BRAN MUFFINS 2(D)           USENET Cookbook       64
012:  [ 524] (cmns-moon.think)  AMBROSIA(D)                 USENET Cookbook       46
013:  [ 512] (cmns-moon.think)  CHOC PUDDING 2(D)           USENET Cookbook       08
014:  [ 512] (cmns-moon.think)  BREAKFAST CAS(M)            USENET Cookbook       73
015:  [ 512] (cmns-moon.think)  BREAD-STUFF-1(S)            USENET Cookbook       71
016:  [ 500] (cmns-moon.think)  TRIFLE-1(D)                 USENET Cookbook       64
017:  [ 500] (cmns-moon.think)  SODA-BREAD(B)               USENET Cookbook       79
018:  [ 500] (cmns-moon.think)  OATMEALCAKES(M)             USENET Cookbook       45


<space> selects, arrows move, w for keywords, s for sources, ? for help
```

3. To look at a document that WAIS finds, move the cursor to the desired document with the cursor keys, or type the line number and press Enter.

4. Press the spacebar to retrieve the document.

5. The document is displayed a page at a time. Press the spacebar to move from page to page or q to stop displaying the document.

6. After displaying as many documents as you want, press s to prepare for another search or q to exit.

TIP

To e-mail a copy of a document to yourself, press | (vertical bar), type **mail *name@host*,** where *name@host* is your e-mail address, and press Enter. After you do that for the first time in a session, WAIS remembers the command so you only need to press | and Enter.

Using WAIS via the World Wide Web

Using WAIS via the World Wide Web (WWW) is often easier than using it directly. Start a WWW client (such as Lynx, as described earlier in this part) at Web page http://www.WAIS.com/directory-of-servers.html. Doing so takes you to a page of WAIS sources; you select the source you want to get a page that contains a field into which you type your search terms. Then press Enter to do the search and receive a page listing all the documents that match. You can select any documents that look interesting to receive the documents themselves.

xarchie

If you are using a graphical system such as Motif, you can use xarchie.

1. Run xarchie. The window shown in the following figure appears.

2. If the standard sub search mode isn't satisfactory, click Search Type and choose the desired type from the menu.

3. Move the cursor to the Search Term box and type the search string there.

4. Click Query to perform the search. xarchie displays the results in three columns.

5. To see the files and directories found in a system name in the first column, click the system name. xarchie displays the names in the second column.

6. To see the files and subdirectories found in a directory name in the second column, click the directory name.

Retrieving files with xarchie

Unlike other versions of Archie, xarchie can retrieve the files it has found.

1. Normally, files are retrieved to the current directory. To use another directory, choose Settings... to get the settings window shown in the following figure.

2. Move the cursor to Local Ftp Directory: setting and type the directory name. Click Done.

3. To retrieve the displayed file(s), click FTP. xarchie retrieves the file.

xgopher

xgopher is a graphic user interface for Gopher. If you are using a graphical system such as Motif, you can use xgopher.

✦ To start xgopher, type **xgopher** in a shell window or select it from a menu if one is available. You see the screen shown in the following figure.

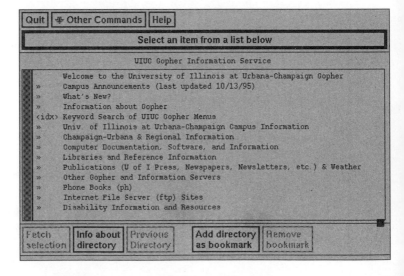

+ To select an item on a menu, click it and then click the Fetch Selection menu button; or just double-click the item.

+ To leave xgopher, click Quit.

 If an xgopher menu doesn't fit in the window, click the left or right mouse button in the gray scroll bar at the left of the window to scroll up or down.

Saving or printing files that xgopher finds

If you select a file item, xgopher opens a window in which you can view that file. You can then save or print the file.

1. To scroll the file up and down, click the Page down and Page up menu buttons, or click the mouse buttons in the scroll bar at the left side of the window.

2. To save the file, click Save To File, move the mouse to the filename box in the Save to file window, type the filename to use, and click OK.

3. To print the file, click Print.

4. To stop viewing the file and close the file's window, click Done.

 You can leave file windows open and return to the main xgopher window. Doing so lets you open several file windows at once. If several windows are open, move the mouse cursor to the window you want to work with.

Searching for information by using xgopher

If you can't find the information you are looking for by moving around the menus (as described earlier in this section), try searching. In xgopher, menu items that can be searched are indicated by <idx>.

1. Select the item by double-clicking it.

2. When xgopher opens the Index Search window, move the cursor to the empty box and type one or more search terms.

3. Click Do Index. xgopher performs the search and creates a menu of items that satisfy the search.

Using xgopher to telnet

If you find something interesting in xgopher and it says that you have to telnet to another system to see it, xgopher offers to telnet for you automatically. On xgopher menus, telnet items end with <tel>.

1. Click a <tel> item. xgopher telnets to a remote system.

2. xgopher may first display a window telling you the user name and password to use. Click OK.

3. A window opens for the telnet session. If necessary, log in with the user name and password provided.

4. Use the system to find the information you want.

5. Log out of the remote system. The telnet window closes.

You can continue using xgopher while the telnet window is open by moving the cursor to the xgopher window. You can even have several telnet windows open at once to different hosts.

Using bookmarks

You can tell xgopher to place a bookmark at a particular menu or item for later reference:

✦ To put a bookmark on an item, click the item and then click Add Selection as Bookmark.

✦ To put a bookmark on the current menu, click in a blank area of the xgopher window and then click Add Directory as Bookmark.

The current bookmarks are displayed in a menu in the lower part of the xgopher window. To select a bookmark, double-click its item in the lower window. To delete a bookmark, click once on its entry in the lower window and then click Remove Bookmark. Regular Gopher and xgopher use the same bookmark file, so bookmarks saved in one program can be used later in the other.

Usenet Newsgroups

Usenet, also known as *network news* or *netnews,* is a gigantic, bulletin-board system distributed worldwide. Usenet is made up of more than 10,000 *newsgroups,* each of which features a discussion on a specific topic. Several UNIX newsreading programs (including `trn`, `nn`, and `tin`) are popular. This part describes how to read Usenet newsgroups by using `trn`.

In this part...

- ✔ Finding and subscribing to newsgroups
- ✔ Finding articles on specific topics
- ✔ Reading, posting, and saving articles
- ✔ Skipping over offensive articles
- ✔ Getting help

Avoiding Getting Flamed (Netiquette)

The list of mail etiquette rules listed at the end of Part II apply equally to news articles — more so, because far more people read news articles than read a piece of e-mail. Here are some other rules:

✦ Don't post a follow-up to the whole group if the follow-up is intended only for the author of the original article.

✦ Be sure that each article is appropriate for the group to which you post it.

✦ Don't post a two-line follow-up that quotes an entire hundred-line article. Edit down the quoted material.

✦ Most groups have a periodic Frequently Asked Questions (or *FAQs*) message that answers many of the questions that you may ask. Check for a FAQ message before asking. (If you have access to FTP, all FAQ messages are available on the system rtfm.mit.edu.)

Changing the Order in Which Newsgroups Appear

You can control the order in which trn presents groups. If you tell trn to present the most interesting ones first, you can move quickly through your favorite groups with the spacebar and n. When you run out of time, you can quit the program, skipping the less interesting newsgroups.

The first newsgroup you usually see is called *general,* and this group is supposed to contain articles of general interest on your machine. In practice, newsgroup *general* tends to fill up with junk, and you should move newsgroup *general* toward the end of your list of groups.

1. Press m (which stands for *move*).

2. If you want to move the current newsgroup, press Enter. To move some other group, type the group's name and press Enter. The program asks you where you want to move the group by displaying the cryptic prompt [$^Lq].

3. If you want to see a list of the newsgroups to which you are subscribed (or have ever been subscribed to), press L (capitalized). You see a list of newsgroups.

4. Press the spacebar when the program pauses at the bottom of the screen. At the end of the listing, you see the same cryptic prompt.

✦ To move the group to the end of the list (so that the group is the last one that you see), press $.

✦ To move the group to the head of the list so that that group is the first one that you see, press ^ (a carat, usually Shift+6).

✦ To move the group so that it appears after another group, press +, type the name of the other group, and then press Enter.

Choosing Which New Newsgroups to Subscribe to

Because Usenet is exploding in popularity, a bunch of new newsgroups appear every day. When you start rn or trn, you see a list of the new newsgroups, and you have the opportunity to subscribe to them. Here's how:

1. Run trn or rn. It asks a question such as this:

```
Checking active list for new newsgroups...
Newsgroup alt.comp.hardware.homebuilt not in
.newsrc-subscribe? [ynYN]
```

2. Press y or n to tell the program whether you want to subscribe to that particular newsgroup.

3. If you do want to subscribe to that newsgroup, the program then asks where in the list of newsgroups you'd like to see this new newsgroup, such as this:

```
Put newsgroup where? [$^L]
```

4. Press $ to put the new newsgroup at the end of your list of newsgroups, or press + followed by the name of an existing group to tell the program to put the new newsgroup after that particular existing group.

If you don't want to hear about any of the new newsgroups, press N (capitalized) to skip all of them.

Dealing with rot-13 Articles

Offensive articles are sometimes encoded using rot-13, a simple coding system. If you encounter an article that contains gibberish, assume that the article has been encoded by someone using rot-13.

1. Decide whether you want to read the article. (You can usually tell what the subject is from the subject line, which is not encoded.)

2. Skip the article by pressing n, or press X to go ahead and pollute your soul.

Dealing with shar Files

Some messages contain groups of files, most often a group of C-program files in *shar* (*shell archive*) format. Extract files in this format with e in exactly the same way that you extract uuencoded files (*see* "Dealing with Unencoded Files," in this part).

Dealing with Uuencoded Files

Some files contain encoded binary data, such as pictures or executable programs. Such messages contain lines that look like this:

```
begin plugh.exe 644
M390GNM4L-REP3PT45G00I-05[I5-
   6M3OME,MRMK760PI5LPTMETLMKPY
MEOT39I4905B05YOPV3OIXKRTL5KWLJROJTOU,6P5;3;MRU05OI4J5OI4
```

This type of format is called *uuencoded* format.

Before you can use this information, you must *extract* it.

1. Display the text of the article.

2. Press e and then press Enter. If you want the data someplace other than your News directory, type the directory name after the e.

3. If the file is large and is split across multiple messages, press e in each message in order.

Exiting the Newsreader

When you are bored by reading messages from computer nerds from all over the world or realize that the time is almost 5:00 and you haven't gotten any useful work done all day, it's time to leave your newsreader.

To do so, press q. Depending on where in the program you are, you may have to press q two or three times.

Finding Articles on Specific Topics

trn and rn can search for articles that contain a specific word or phrase or part of a word.

1. While you are reading a newsgroup, press a slash followed by the characters you want to search for. For example, to find information about chickens, type **/chickens**.

2. The program displays the next article that contains the characters you type. If the program doesn't find an article that contains those characters, it tells you so.

If you want to scan backward through the articles, press ? rather than / before the characters you want to search for.

You can tell the program what to scan: either just the headers or the whole article (which takes longer). To scan only the *From* lines (which say who posted the article), type

/pattern/f

where *pattern* is the characters you are searching for.

To scan only lines in the header, but not lines in the text of the articles, type

/pattern/h

To scan entire articles, type

/pattern/a

To scan articles that you have already read, type

/pattern/r

To match the capitalization of the pattern you are searching for, type

/pattern/c

Finding a Newsgroup

When trn or rn asks whether you want to read a newsgroup, you can read the articles in a different newsgroup instead. To read the messages of a particular newsgroup, you use the g (goto) command.

1. When the program asks whether you want to read a newsgroup, press g (and don't press Enter).

2. Type the name of the newsgroup.

3. Press Enter. Your newsreader subscribes you to the newsgroup.

If you have unsubscribed to a newsgroup and want to resubscribe to it, this command does so.

To find a newsgroup of interest to you, read either news.announce.newgroups or news.announce.newusers newsgroups; both contain complete listings of all the newsgroups.

Getting Help

trn and rn don't have the world's finest online help, but their online help is sometimes better than nothing. While trn is asking you whether you want to read a newsgroup, you see a list of the newsgroup selection commands. While you are looking at the list of threads in a newsgroup, you see the list of thread-selection commands. While you are reading articles, you see a list of commands that control the way articles appear.

1. To see the newsreader's online help, press h. You see a terse listing of commands, one per line.

2. The listing of commands is too long to fit on one screen. Press the spacebar to see the next page.

Posting a New Article

You can start your own thread by posting an article. Just make sure that the article is on an interesting topic, that the newsgroup hasn't just discussed that topic at length last week, and that you have your facts straight.

Before posting an article, be sure that you have read the newsgroup for at least a week so that you know which topics the newsgroup is discussing and what the style of the newsgroup is; that you have read the newsgroup's FAQ; and that you are calm or (even better) in a good mood.

1. Within trn or rn, enter the newsgroup of interest.

2. If you're in the thread-selection screen, press Enter to go the article-reading screen (trn only).

3. Press j to tell the program that you're not reading any articles.

4. Press f (as though you were writing a follow-up article to something).

5. The program asks whether you're sure that you want to write an article. If you are sure, press y and press Enter.

6. When prompted to, enter a new subject for the article.

7. Write the new article the same way that you'd write a follow-up (as described in the section "Replying to and Following Up an Article").

If you're not running rn or trn at the moment, you can use the Pnews command to post news directly. At the command prompt, type **Pnews** followed by the name of the newsgroup to post to. Then follow the directions given in this part for posting an article.

Some newsgroups are *moderated*, which means that articles are not posted directly as news. Instead, articles are e-mailed to a human moderator who actually posts the articles if they are appropriate to the group. Moderators, being human, do not process items instantaneously, so processing items can take a day or two. If you write an article for a moderated group, the news-posting software tells you that your article is being mailed to the moderator.

Reading Articles

After you choose a newsgroup to read (by pressing the spacebar when trn asks whether you want to read the messages in the group), trn shows you the first screen of the first unread article. You can read each article that you haven't read yet, skip over articles that look boring, reply to messages, print them, or save them.

A group of messages that have the same subject is called a *thread*. If a subject looks boring, you can tell trn to skip entire threads:

1. To read the messages in a newsgroup, press the spacebar when trn asks whether to read them.

You see the first message that you have not read, such as this:

```
general #6281
From: Admin
Re: Disk space
Organization: I.E.C.C.
Date: Sat Aug  7 06:48:03 1996
The disks are nearly full again. Please delete unneeded
files, or we'll delete some for you.
(Yes, that's a threat.) — Your friendly system manager
End of article 6281 (of 6282)—what next? [npq]
```

2. If the article is too long to fit on-screen, press the spacebar to see the next screen of the article.

3. To see the next article in this newsgroup, press n. If you don't feel like reading any of the unread articles in the newsgroup, press c to *catch up* — pretend that you've read all the articles. If you have finished reading articles in this newsgroup, press q.

The first line of the article tells you the name of the newsgroup (*general*) and the message number within the group (6281). The last line tells you how many articles are in the newsgroup (6282, in this case) and which one you are looking at again (6281, which means that one more unread message is in this newsgroup).

After you get the hang of it, you'll mostly press the spacebar to go to the next article or newsgroup, n to skip an article or newsgroup, and k to skip a group of articles (as described in the next section). Until you prune the set of newsgroups you're subscribed to down to something reasonable, you may also be hitting u frequently to get rid of the large majority of groups that you don't want to read.

Key to Use While Reading an Article	Meaning
Spacebar	Read the next page of the current article or the next unread article.
B	Back up a page.
n	Skip to the next article.
k	Kill this article and any others with the same title.
K	Same as k; also enter the title in the killfile so that the title is rekilled each time you enter the group.
q	Leave this group.
c	Catch up (pretend that you've read all articles in this group).
u	Unsubscribe to this newsgroup.
s*pdq*	Save article to a file named *pdq*.
| *lpr*	Feed article to command *lpr* (this method is the easiest way to print an article).
/*xyz*	Find the next article whose title contains *xyz*.
=	Show titles of unread articles.
Ctrl+L	Redraw the screen.
Ctrl+R	Restart the current article (redisplays the first page).
X	Unscramble rot-13 message (not for the squeamish).
e	Extract uudecoded or shar file.
e*dir*	Extract into directory *dir*.
h	Show extremely concise help.
q	Leave this group.

Replying to and Following Up an Article

You can write a response to an article in two different ways:

✦ You can send e-mail, known as a *reply,* to the article's author. The other folks in the newsgroup won't see your reply because your reply is a private e-mail message.

✦ You can write an article of your own to the newsgroup at large; this process is known as *posting a follow-up article.* Post a follow-up article only if you are sure that most of the people in the newsgroup may find your response interesting.

Sending an e-mail reply

1. While the original article is still open, press r. If you want to include some or all of the text of the article in your reply, press R instead.

2. trn or rn starts a text editor (usually vi or emacs) with a skeleton of the reply message already provided. If you press R, the text editor includes a copy of the original article with your reply.

3. Type your reply. If you are starting your message with the original article, delete the irrelevant parts of the article.

4. Save the file and exit the text editor.

5. trn or rn asks whether you want to send, abort, or edit the response. To send the message, press s. If you change your mind, press a to abort the reply and not send anything.

6. The program then asks whether it should add your standard signature (stored in your file .signature). Press y unless you have already signed the article.

Posting a news follow-up

1. Press f to send a follow-up. If you want to include some or all of the text of the article in your follow-up, press F instead.

2. The program asks whether you're sure that you want to send a follow-up to the whole Net. If you're sure that's what you want to do, press y.

3. trn or rn starts a text editor, with a skeleton of the follow-up message already provided. If you press F, it includes a copy of the original article.

4. Type your follow-up. If you started with the original article, delete the irrelevant parts.

5. Save the file and leave the text editor.

6. The program asks whether to send the follow-up. Press y to send the follow-up or press a to abort and not send it.

All news articles that you send, including follow-ups, automatically add your .signature file. Don't put in the signature yourself, or your signature will appear twice.

Saving an Article

Just like mail messages, newsgroup articles can be saved in files.

1. To save an article that you are reading, press s followed by the name of the file in which to save it; then press Enter.

2. If the file doesn't already exist, trn or rn asks whether to make the file a mailbox. To make the file a mailbox, press y.

If you don't specify a directory, trn or rn saves articles in files or mailboxes in your News directory. You can put articles in other directories by specifying the directory name, but News is usually as good a place as any.

Selecting Newsgroups to Read

After you begin running trn or rn, you choose which newsgroups to read (unless you've decided to follow all 10,000 of them). When you see a message such as 23 unread articles in soc.couples-read now? [+ynq], press one of the keys listed in the following table:

Key	Meaning
Spacebar or y	Enter the next group that has unread articles (described in "Reading Articles," in this part).
+	Display a list of the threads that contain unread articles (trn only).
n	Skip this group for now (see "Skipping over a Newsgroup," later in this part).
u	Unsubscribe from this group so that you won't see it any more (**see** "Unsubscribing to a Newsgroup," later in this part).
g	Go to a different newsgroup; type the newsgroup name after the g (**see** "Finding a Newsgroup," in this part).
q	Leave trn or rn.
p	Go to the previous group with unread news.
h	Show extremely concise help.
Ctrl+L	Redraw the screen.

Selecting the Threads That You Want to Read

After you tell `trn` or `rn` to enter a newsgroup, so many articles may be in the newsgroup that even killing and junking them still leaves too many to read. Instead of reading all the articles, you can select only those subjects that you *do* want to see.

`trn` has a feature called *thread selection* that makes this selection easy, but `rn` doesn't have this feature. Follow these steps to use it:

1. Enter the desired newsgroup by pressing + (instead of the usual spacebar or y). You see a screen such as this:

```
general                        14 articles
a 0000-uucp(0000)    3  New mail paths
b 0000-Admin(0000) 10  backup
d Chet Arthur        1  System will down to clean ham-
   ster cages —
Select threads — All [Z>] —
```

The first line tells you the newsgroup's name and the number of articles in the newsgroup. The following lines list the threads with a one-letter identifier (for example, *d*), the author of the first article in the thread (*Chet Arthur*), the number of messages in the thread (*1*), and the subject (*System will down to clean hamster cages*). The last line asks which thread you want to read.

2. Press the appropriate letters (the one letter identifiers) to select the threads that you want. To select a range of threads, press the letter of the first thread followed by a hyphen and the letter of the last thread.

3. To go to the next page of threads, press > (right-arrow key).

4. To start reading the threads that you've selected, press Z or Tab.

If you want to read all the threads on the current screen, simply press Z or Tab without selecting any of them.

To *junk* (arrange never to see) the threads that aren't selected, press D. The most effective way to pick just the articles of interest is to select the interesting threads on each screen by using the key letters and then press D to quickly skip the rest of the threads on that screen.

The spacebar is set up to pick the command that you are most likely to want at the end of each screen. If another screen of threads is available, the spacebar does the same as > to go to the next screen. On the last screen, pressing the spacebar does the same as pressing Z to start reading articles.

Thread Key Selection Letter	Meaning
Spacebar	Read the next page of the table of contents or start reading selected articles if no more threads are in the table of contents.
D	Start reading selected articles; mark unselected articles as read.
Z	Read selected articles.
/xyz	Select articles whose titles contain *xyz*.
c-g	Select articles *c* through *g* in the current table of contents.
c	Catch up, by pretending that you've read every article in the group (available in recent versions of t rn only).
h	Show extremely concise help.
q	Leave this group.

Skipping Over a Newsgroup

When trn asks whether you want to read a newsgroup now, you can skip over the newsgroup just this once. To skip a group for the time being, press n to say, "No, don't read it now." You remain subscribed to the newsgroup.

Skipping an Uninteresting or Offensive Article

Often, you find an article to be uninteresting enough that you want to skip it, skip all the replies, and perhaps skip every future reply as well.

+ To skip (kill) this article and all others with the same subject, press k (lowercase k).

+ To curse this subject permanently and skip it in the future as well, press K (capital K).

+ To skip (junk) the rest of this thread, even if the subject changes, press J.

Pressing k, K, or J adds a command to one of your *killfiles,* that is, the files that store information about what types of articles you want to skip in the future. Press Ctrl+K to edit the killfile for the current newsgroup.

Skipping Unread Articles

When you are reading articles in the newsgroup, press c (for *catch up*) to mark all the unread articles in this newsgroup as read. If hundreds of unread articles are in a newsgroup that you follow, you may want to mark them all as read so that you don't have to face them.

Starting Your Newsreader

In nearly all newsreading programs, you don't need to press Enter (or Return) after single-letter commands. Other commands require that you type a line of text, such as a filename or a newsgroup name, after the letter. In that case, you do press Enter to tell the program that you're done with the line of text. Be sure that you use either capital or small letters for one-letter commands *just as they are shown in the book* — the same letter can do different things depending on whether that letter is capitalized or not!

1. Run the trn program.

2. If the system says that the trn program is not found, run rn instead.

When you run the program for the first time, it creates your .newsrc file and automatically subscribes you to some groups. You see something like this:

```
% trn Trying to set up a .newsrc file—running
    newsetup... Creating .newsrc in /usr/johnl to be
    used by news programs.
Done. If you have never used the news system before,
    you may find the articles in news.announce.newusers
    to be helpful. There is also a manual entry for
    rn. To get rid of newsgroups you aren't interested
    in, use the 'u' command.
Type h for help at any time while running rn.
Unread news in general
    14 articles
(Revising soft pointers—be patient.)
Unread news in ne.food
    47 articles
Unread news in ne.forsale
    1177 articles
Unread news in ne.general
    268 articles
etc. ********  14 unread articles in general—read now?
    [+ynq]
```

Your newsreader now suggests a newsgroup for you to read.

trn (or rn) keeps a list of the newsgroups that you are interested in (that is, that you are *subscribed to*). If you are not interested in a newsgroup, you can *unsubscribe*. When new newsgroups are created, trn asks whether you want to subscribe to them.

To start, trn assumes that you are subscribed to some or all newsgroups, depending on how your news administrator configured the program. You unsubscribe to those newsgroups you don't care about. After the very first time you run trn, you don't see the first few lines of the preceding example; you see just the list of newsgroups to which you are subscribed and the number of unread messages in each. If you are subscribed to a whole bunch of newsgroups (more than about five), the program lists only the first few.

Understanding Newsgroup Names

Usenet newsgroups are named according to a hierarchy. They consist of several parts separated by dots — for example, rec.food.chocolate. The first part of the name (rec, in this example) determines which *hierarchy* the newsgroup belongs to and describes the general subject area. The following table lists the most widely read subjects:

Newsgroup Name	Description
comp	Topics having something to do with computers.
sci	Topics having something to do with the sciences.
rec	Recreational groups (about sports, hobbies, the arts, and other fun endeavors).
soc	Social groups (both social interests and plain socializing).
news	Topics having to do with Usenet itself. A few groups contain general announcements; otherwise they're not very interesting unless you're a Usenet addict.
misc	Miscellaneous topics that don't fit anywhere else. (The ultimate miscellaneous group is called misc.misc.)
talk	Long arguments, frequently political. Widely considered totally uninteresting except to the participants.
alt	Unofficial *alternative* newsgroups, ranging from the topical to the weird to the totally stupid.

Regional and organizational hierarchies also exist. For example, the ne hierarchy is for topics of interest to New England, ny is for New York, and ba is for the San Francisco Bay area. Universities and other organizations big enough to have their own Usenet communities often have hierarchies of their own, such as mit for M.I.T.

You can see the list of newsgroups available on your system by looking at /usr/lib/news/active.

See *The Internet For Dummies,* 3rd Edition (IDG Books Worldwide, Inc.) for more information about Usenet newsgroups.

Unsubscribing to a Newsgroup

When trn asks whether you want to read a newsgroup, you can tell trn that you never want to hear about the newsgroup again. To unsubscribe from a group, press u.

Techie Talk

absolute pathname: A pathname that tells you how to find a file by starting at the root directory and working down the directory tree.

address: The name you use to say who is supposed to receive an electronic-mail message. An electronic-mail address consists of the person's user name and, if on a different computer than you are, the name of the computer.

Alt key: If your keyboard has an Alt key, it is used as a Shift key; it does nothing on its own. To use the Alt key, hold it down, press and release another key, and release the Alt key. To press Alt+A, for example, hold the Alt key, press and release the A key, and release the Alt key. Simple. Lacking an Alt key, you can usually press Esc and then the letter to get the same effect.

anonymous FTP: Uses the FTP file transfer program and the Internet to copy files from other computers to your own. It is *anonymous* because many computer systems allow anyone to log in and transfer files without having accounts (user names) on the computer. You type **anonymous** as the user name and your electronic-mail address as the password.

application: A program that really gets some work done. Some programs just organize the computer, get its parts talking to each other, and do other housekeeping chores. Application programs do real-world work, such as word processing or accounting.

argument: Something that appears on a command line after the command. Suppose you type this line:

```
cp old.file new.file
```

In this command, `cp` is the name of the command or program, `old.file` is the first argument, and `new.file` is the second argument.

ASCII (American Standard Code for Information Interchange): ASCII defines the codes that the computer uses internally to store letters, numbers, punctuation, and some control codes. Almost all UNIX computers use ASCII (except for some IBM mainframes).

background: UNIX can run many programs at the same time. If a program runs behind the scenes — that is, with no interaction with you — it runs in the background.

backslash (\): UNIX uses a backslash to set off otherwise-special characters. In the UNIX shell, for example, `\*` is a literal asterisk (a plain `*` matches every file in the current directory); `\\` is an actual backslash. DOS users tend to type backslashes by mistake when UNIX would rather see a regular slash (/).

bang (!): In UNIX-ese, an exclamation point is called a *bang*. The C shell command `!!`, for example, which repeats the last command, is pronounced "Bang! Bang!" Try this with your small children — they'll love it.

BASH: The Bourne Again shell, the GNU re-creation of the Bourne shell. Program name is `bash`.

bin: A directory that contains programs. Your home directory probably has a subdirectory named `bin`. The system has directories called `/bin` and `/usr/bin`.

bit: A tiny piece of information that can be either a 1 or a 0. Bits tend to get lumped into groups of eight bits, called *bytes*.

Bourne shell: The Bourne shell is the most widely used UNIX shell. It prompts you with $. Its program name is `sh`.

Break key: You use the Break key before you log in when you are dialing on a modem to tell UNIX that it has guessed wrong about which kind of modem you're using. You may have to press Break two or three times until you get a proper `login:` message. Some keyboards have a key labeled Break. If yours doesn't, and you're using a PC with a modem program, try Alt+B or check your modem program's help screen.

BSD UNIX: A version of UNIX developed and distributed by the University of California at Berkeley. BSD stands for *Berkeley Software Distribution.*

buffer: A small storage area in which information is stored temporarily until it is needed. Lots of things have buffers: printers frequently have buffers to store the next few lines or pages to print; `emacs` (a text editor) refers to its copies of the files you are editing as buffers.

byte: Eight bits in a row. That is, a series of eight pieces of information, each of which can be either 1 or 0. A little higher math tells you that there are 256 different combinations of eight 1s and 0s. (256 is 2 to the 8th power.) There are, therefore, 256 different values for a byte of information. Most computers use a system of codes called *ASCII* to determine what each pattern means. *See also* ASCII.

C: A programming language, invented at the same time as UNIX, in which nearly all UNIX programs are written. C is a great programming language for lots of reasons. C programs look a lot like random punctuation strewn across the page. Luckily, you do *not* have to know C to use UNIX, so we don't write about it anywhere else in this book.

C shell: The C shell is a UNIX shell written to look like the C programming language, sort of. It prompts you with %. Its program name is `csh`.

CD-ROM: A computer disc that looks just like a music CD but contains data rather than music.

click-to-type: A system that GUIs *(graphical user interfaces)* use to control which window you are working in. When you want to move to a different window, move the mouse and click the new window to tell the GUI that you want to use that window.

client: In X Windows, a program that does real work (as opposed to a program that displays the results on-screen).

client-server architecture: A system (used by X) that enables a program (the *client*) to run on one machine while the program that displays its results (the *server*) runs on another machine. Confusingly, it is also used in the database world to mean when a presentation or analysis program (the client) runs on one machine and the database engine (the server) runs on another computer.

command: What you type to get UNIX to do something. Actually, the *UNIX shell* listens to the commands you type and tries to execute them. Some commands are things the shell knows how to do. Other commands are separate programs, stored in files on the disk. When you type a command, press Enter or Return at the end of the line.

command mode: When you use the `ed` or `vi` text editors, you are in either command mode or input mode. In command mode, whatever you type is interpreted as a command.

compression: A way to shrink files so that they don't take up so much space. File-compression programs that do this include `compress` and `pack`. To uncompress a compressed file, use `uncompress`, `unpack`, or `zcat`.

Control key: The key on the keyboard labeled *Control* or *Ctrl*. It is used as a Shift key; it does nothing on its own. To use the Ctrl key, hold it down, press and release another key, and release the Ctrl key. To press Ctrl+D, for example, hold down the Ctrl key, press and release the D key, and release the Ctrl key.

.cshrc: The file that the C shell runs automatically when it starts.

current directory: *See* working directory.

current job: The job most recently started or stopped. When you use the `jobs` command to list jobs, the current job is marked with a plus sign (+).

daemon: A process that runs around on its own to see to some housekeeping task. Your computer, or some computer on your network, has a printer daemon whose job is to print things waiting in the print queue.

directory: A collection of files with a name. A directory can be compared to a file folder that contains one or more files. Directories can also contain other directories. You can think of a directory as a work area because one directory is always the current *working directory*. Directories, particularly directories contained in your home directory, sometimes are called *subdirectories,* for no good reason.

DOS: An operating system patterned in some ways after UNIX. DOS runs on PCs.

dumb terminal: A terminal that has no processing power of its own. It usually doesn't have any nice options either, such as mice or screens that can do graphics.

editor: *See* text editor.

electronic mail (or e-mail or email): Typed messages sent on a computer network rather than on paper.

Enter key: In a UNIX shell, pressing Enter means that you have just typed a command and want UNIX to do it. In a text editor, pressing Enter means that you want to begin a new line. The Enter and Return keys usually do the same thing (your keyboard may have one, the other, or both).

Escape key: The key labeled *Escape* or *Esc*. What this key does depends on the program you are using.

executable file: A file that UNIX can run like a program. An executable file can contain binary machine instructions that the computer knows how to execute, or it can contain a *shell script* (a list of UNIX shell commands) that UNIX knows how to execute.

external command: A command that the shell doesn't actually know how to do. Instead, a program is stored in a file with the same name as the command. If you type the ed command (to run the dreadful ed editor), for example, UNIX runs the program contained by a file named ed.

file: A bunch of information stored together with a name. A file can contain text, programs, or data in any format.

file system: A set of files stored on a disk or on one partition of a disk. A file system has one root directory that contains files and subdirectories. These subdirectories can, in turn, contain files and other directories.

file transfer: Copying files from one computer to another.

filter: A small UNIX program used with input or output redirection. The most commonly used filters are the more and sort commands.

flag: *See* option.

folder: A file that contains electronic-mail messages that you have decided to save.

foreground: A program currently capable of talking to your terminal.

fork: When UNIX starts a new process, it does so by cloning an existing process. The cloning process is known in UNIX-ese as *forking*. Pronounce it carefully to avoid embarrassment.

FTP: A file-transfer program that enables you to log in to another computer and transfer files to or from your computer.

GUI: A graphical *user* interface. GUIs let you use the computer by pointing at things with a mouse rather than typing commands. The most common UNIX GUI is Motif. GUIs sometimes are called *windowing systems*.

header: The first part of an electronic-mail message that contains the address of the sender and recipient, the subject, and lots of other stuff that is less interesting.

hidden file: A file with a filename that begins with a period. These files do not appear on regular ls directory listings. Use ls -a to include hidden files in a directory listing.

home directory: The directory you start in when you log in, usually a subdirectory of /usr. You should keep your files in your home directory or in subdirectories of your home directory.

icon: A cute little picture used in conjunction with a GUI. A well-designed icon is supposed to be an obvious, unmistakable symbol of whatever it stands for, occupy much less space than do the equivalent words, and be cute. In practice, many icons are peculiar little pictures with no obvious meaning.

inbox: *See* mailbox.

incremental backup: A backup copy of only the files that have changed since the last full backup.

input mode: When you use the ed or vi text editors, you are in either command mode or input mode. In input mode, whatever you type is entered into the file.

Internet: A large and growing set of interconnected computer networks to which many UNIX systems are directly or indirectly connected.

I/O: Input and output, that is, information going into or coming out of a program, computer, or other computer-type device.

I/O redirection: *See* redirection.

job: A program you start from the shell that can start, stop, and move between the foreground and background.

K (also KB or kilobyte): A measure of memory or disk size that is 1,024 bytes of information. This number happens to be 2 multiplied by itself 10 times — a nice, round number for computers.

kill: To stop a process from running.

kludge: Something that works but that the author is embarrassed about. Rhymes with "huge," not with "fudge." Some people spell it *kluge,* and we're sure that they too can learn to live productive and useful lives.

Korn shell: An enhanced version of the Bourne shell. For your purposes, it's mostly like the Bourne shell and prompts you with a $. Its program name is ksh.

line editor: A text editor that deals with text one line at a time. Most modern text editors let you see and work with the file an entire screen at a time. The ed program is a line editor; we recommend that you use something better.

link: An additional name for a file. When you create a file, you create its contents, which are stored on the disk, and you give it a name, which is stored in a directory. There is a connection between the filename and its contents. You can create additional filenames and connect them to the same contents by using the ln command.

Linux: A free version of UNIX originally written by Linus Torvalds in Finland and now developed by a cast of thousands all over the world, connected by the Internet.

local mount: Logically connects several disk drives on the same machine so that they appear as one file system.

log in: To identify yourself to the UNIX system and provide your password so that UNIX believes that it's really you and lets you use the computer. You have a login ID, or user ID, or user name — that is, the name by which UNIX knows you. When you finish working, you log out.

.login: A hidden file containing a shell script. If you use the C shell, this script runs automatically every time you log in.

login directory: *See* home directory.

Lynx: A Web browser that runs under UNIX. Lynx doesn't display any pictures, but the text looks great.

MB, M, or megabyte: Measure of memory and disk size that is 1,048,576 bytes, or 1K times 1K, or 2 multiplied by itself 20 times.

mailbox: The directory in which the electronic-mail system puts your incoming mail.

man page: A short file of information about a UNIX command. The man command displays manual pages about all UNIX commands and a few other topics, although they usually are written in a hopelessly technoid style.

Meta key: If your keyboard has an Alt key, it is also the Meta key. If not, press the Escape key to achieve the same effect. The effect depends on the program you are running. emacs uses the Meta key for many commands.

MIME (Multipurpose Internet Mail Extensions): A way to attach any kind of file to an e-mail message.

Motif: A GUI based on X Windows and distributed by the Open Software Foundation.

mounting directories: Logically attaching the root directory of one file system to some other directory so that you can treat all the files in the file system as though they were subdirectories. Mounts can be *local* (on the same machine) or *remote* (on a different machine).

netiquette: Rules of polite behavior for sending electronic mail.

network: A bunch of computers connected by some combination of cables, phone lines, satellites, or whatever. A network enables computers (and their users) to share information and peripherals.

Networks are especially good for sharing printers (so that you can all share one good-but-expensive laser printer) and for passing around electronic mail.

NeXTstep: An extremely cool GUI that runs on NeXT machines.

NFS (Network File System): A network system that lets you treat files on another computer in more or less the same way that you treat files on your own computer.

NIS (Network Information System): A database containing the user names, machine names, and directory names that an NFS uses to give consistent names on all machines on a network.

OPEN LOOK: A GUI based on X Windows and developed by AT&T. Most people use Motif instead.

operating system: A special program that controls the way the computer, keyboard, screen, and disks work together. UNIX is an operating system, as is DOS.

option: Also known as a *flag* or *switch*, an option is something that tells UNIX how to do a command. You type an option on the command line after the name of the command, separated from the command by a space. All options begin with a dash (-).

parent directory: The directory that contains the current working directory. That is, the current working directory is a subdirectory of the parent directory.

password: A secret series of characters known only to you. You type your password when you log in.

pathname: Instructions for how to get to a file. An *absolute pathname* tells you how to find a file beginning at the root directory and working down the directory tree. A *relative pathname* tells you how to find the file starting where you are now.

peripheral: Something that lets the computer communicate with the outside world — mainly with you. The keyboard, screen, mouse, printer, and modem all are peripherals.

permissions: Whoever has the right to look at, change, and execute stuff in a file or directory.

pipe: The I character, used to redirect the output of one command so that it becomes the input of another command.

policy independence: A characteristic of X Windows in which windows can look and act any way the software developers want. This idea is the converse of the idea that, if all the windows on your screen look and act in a similar way, they will be easier for you to use.

portable software: Software (programs) that can be run on a number of different kinds of computers. UNIX is portable because it runs on an amazing number of different types of computers.

PostScript: A computer language spoken by printers and the programs that communicate with these printers. PostScript enables printers to print a wonderful array of characters in all kinds of sizes and shapes (as well as pictures). When a program wants to print something on a PostScript printer, it has to send a PostScript program that tells the printer how to print the stuff.

process: A running program.

.profile: A hidden file that contains shell commands. If you use the Bourne or Korn shell, this file runs automatically every time you log in.

prompt: The character or characters displayed whenever UNIX (or some other program) is waiting for you to type something. The two common UNIX prompts are $ (if you use the Bourne or Korn shell) or % (if you use the C shell).

queue: A waiting line, just as in real life. The most common queue is the print queue, in which the output of lp or lpr commands waits in line to get printed.

read-only: A file that can be read (copied and so on) but not written (changed). UNIX has a system of permissions that enables the owner of the file, the owner's group, or all users to have (or not have) permission to read, write, or execute the file.

real-time: Right now, as opposed to whenever the computer gets around to it.

redirection: To hijack the output of a command, which is usually on-screen, and put it somewhere else (this process is called *output redirection*). Alternatively, you can use information from somewhere else as the input for a command (called *input redirection*) rather than take the input from the keyboard. To redirect the output of a command to a file, use the > character. To redirect the input of a command from a file, use the < character. To redirect the output of one command to become the input to another command, use the pipe (|) character.

remote login: Logging in to another computer from your own computer. This process requires that your computer be on a network or have a phone connection.

remote mount: Using NFS to connect directories from disk drives on other machines so that they appear as part of your file system.

request ID: The ID number of a print job as it waits in the print queue for the printer daemon to get around to printing it. You need to know the request ID if you want to cancel printing when, for example, the output is horribly fouled up and wasting lots of paper.

Return key: When you use a UNIX shell, pressing Return means that you have just typed a command and want UNIX to do it. When you use a text editor, pressing Return means that you want to begin a new line. The Enter and Return keys usually do the same thing (your keyboard may have one, the other, or both).

RFS (Remote File System): Like NFS, a program that lets you treat files on another computer in more or less the same way as you treat files on your own computer.

root: *See* superuser.

root directory: The main, top-level directory on a disk. All the files on the disk are in either the root directory or a subdirectory of the root directory (or a sub-subdirectory and so on).

screen editor: A text editor that deals with text an entire screen at a time. The vi and emacs programs are screen editors.

script: *See* shell script.

search path: A list of directories in which UNIX looks for programs.

server: *See* X server.

shar message: An electronic-mail message that contains a shell script that re-creates one or more files when you run it. A clever way to send nontext files through electronic mail.

shell: A UNIX program that listens for commands that you type and tries to execute them. There are several UNIX shells, including the Bourne shell, Korn shell, C shell, and BASH.

shell script: A file that contains a list of UNIX shell commands. You can *run* a shell script, thereby telling UNIX to execute every command in the list.

slash: The / character that UNIX uses in pathnames. A / by itself, or at the beginning of a pathname, means the root directory of the file system. Slashes are used also between one directory name and the next, and between the directory name and the filename in long pathnames.

soft link: A link that contains the name of another file, which may be on another file system. A soft link makes it look as though the file from the other file system is in a directory on your own file system. Also called a *symbolic link*. *See also* link.

subdirectory: *See* directory.

superuser: The user name with which you can do all sorts of dangerous things to the system, including creating new user names and installing new hardware and software. Also known as *root*. With luck, you don't know the password for the superuser. If you do, *use it carefully*. The system administrator really should be the only person who logs in as the superuser.

SVR4: Release 4 (the final version) of UNIX System V from AT&T. Contains more features than any six people would ever want to use.

switch: *See* option.

symbolic link: *See* soft link.

system administrator: The person whose job it is to keep the computer, and possibly the network, running.

System V: A version of UNIX developed and distributed originally by AT&T, later by UNIX System Labs, and now by Novell.

telnet: A program that enables you to log in to another computer from your computer.

terminal: A screen and keyboard connected to a computer somewhere else. The terminal doesn't run UNIX and all those neat programs itself; it just lets you use the computer that does.

terminal emulator: A program that enables a big, powerful computer to act like a dumb, cheap terminal. Commonly, a PC can run a terminal emulator so that you can use another computer running UNIX. UNIX includes a simple terminal emulator called cu.

terminal output stop mode: A terminal setting in which a background job stops if it tries to send anything to your screen.

text editor: A program that lets you create files of text and edit (or change) them. The most common UNIX text editors are ed, vi, and emacs.

text file: A file that contains lines of text. All the stuff in a text file must be ASCII characters — no bizarre control codes, data, programs, or the like. You can use the cat command to look at a text file on-screen. If a file looks like it was written by Martians when you use the cat command to view it, it's not a text file.

text formatter: A program that reads text files and creates nice-looking formatted output. The most common UNIX text formatters are troff, nroff, and TeX.

UNIXWare: Novell's version of UNIX. Descended from SVR4.

Usenet: A very large, very informal, very disorganized network through which many megabytes of news, rumor, and gossip are distributed every day.

user name: The name by which UNIX knows you. You enter this name when you log in. Also known as your *user ID* or *login ID*.

utility: A small, useful program. UNIX comes with some utilities, such as diff and sort.

uucp: The UNIX-to-UNIX copy program. One of the ways that mail, Usenet news, and random files can be sent between computers.

uuencoded file: An electronic-mail message that contains a shell script that, when you run it, re-creates one or more binary files. This is a clever way to send binary files through electronic mail.

virtual memory: A sneaky trick by which UNIX pretends to have more memory than it really does. When you're not looking, UNIX copies information from memory to the disk to free up space in memory. When you need the information on disk, UNIX copies it from the disk back into memory. Virtual memory is generally invisible, except when a program uses it too enthusiastically; then the computer spends all its time copying stuff back and forth to the disk and no time doing useful work, a condition called *thrashing*.

wildcard: A special character that acts like a joker when used in filenames or pathnames. UNIX has two: * and ?.

WIMP: *W*indows, *i*cons, and *m*ouse *p*ointing. *See also* GUI.

window: A rectangular area of the screen in which a program displays something. If you use a GUI, you can have several windows on-screen at a time, each displaying a different program.

window manager: A program (Motif comes with one) that gives the screen the overall look of a GUI.

wizard: A person who knows more about UNIX than is really healthy. Encourage wizards to get outside once in a while.

word processor: A program that lets you create documents — files that contain text, pictures, and formatting codes. UNIX word processors include WordPerfect and Microsoft Word.

working directory: The directory you are working in. The pwd command tells you your working directory.

workstation: A computer with a big screen, a keyboard, and a mouse. If it runs UNIX, it's called a workstation; if it runs DOS, it's called a PC. And if it runs Macintosh Finder (or whatever that system is called), it's called a Mac.

X server: A program that draws the pictures and displays the text on-screen if you use X Windows or a GUI based on X Windows.

X terminal: A terminal that can run X so that you can use X Windows or Motif. It has a little computer in it to do the X stuff.

X window system (or just X): A GUI designed at MIT and based on X.

XENIX: A version of UNIX developed by Microsoft and now maintained and distributed by SCO (Santa Cruz Organization).

Yellow Pages: *See* NIS.

Index

IDG BOOKS WORLDWIDE REGISTRATION CARD

RETURN THIS REGISTRATION CARD FOR FREE CATALOG

Title of this book: UNIX For Dummies QR, 2E

My overall rating of this book: ❑ Very good [1]   ❑ Good [2]   ❑ Satisfactory [3]   ❑ Fair [4]   ❑ Poor [5]

How I first heard about this book:

❑ Found in bookstore; name: [6]

❑ Advertisement: [8]

❑ Word of mouth; heard about book from friend, co-worker, etc.: [10]

❑ Book review: [7]

❑ Catalog: [9]

❑ Other: [11]

What I liked most about this book:

What I would change, add, delete, etc., in future editions of this book:

Other comments:

Number of computer books I purchase in a year: ❑ 1 [12]   ❑ 2-5 [13]   ❑ 6-10 [14]   ❑ More than 10 [15]

I would characterize my computer skills as: ❑ Beginner [16]   ❑ Intermediate [17]   ❑ Advanced [18]   ❑ Professional [19]

I use ❑ DOS [20]   ❑ Windows [21]   ❑ OS/2 [22]   ❑ Unix [23]   ❑ Macintosh [24]   ❑ Other: [25] _____
(please specify)

I would be interested in new books on the following subjects:
(please check all that apply, and use the spaces provided to identify specific software)

❑ Word processing: [26]

❑ Data bases: [28]

❑ File Utilities: [30]

❑ Networking: [32]

❑ Other: [34]

❑ Spreadsheets: [27]

❑ Desktop publishing: [29]

❑ Money management: [31]

❑ Programming languages: [33]

I use a PC at (please check all that apply): ❑ home [35]   ❑ work [36]   ❑ school [37]   ❑ other: [38]

The disks I prefer to use are ❑ 5.25 [39]   ❑ 3.5 [40]   ❑ other: [41]

I have a CD ROM: ❑ yes [42]   ❑ no [43]

I plan to buy or upgrade computer hardware this year: ❑ yes [44]   ❑ no [45]

I plan to buy or upgrade computer software this year: ❑ yes [46]   ❑ no [47]

Name: _____   Business title: [48]

Type of Business: [49]

Address (❑ home [50]   ❑ work [51]/Company name: _____)

Street/Suite#

City [52]/State [53]/Zipcode [54]: _____   Country [55]

❑ **I liked this book!**
You may quote me by name in future IDG Books Worldwide promotional materials.

My daytime phone number is _____

IDG BOOKS

THE WORLD OF
COMPUTER
KNOWLEDGE

❏ YES!

Please keep me informed about IDG's World of Computer Knowledge. Send me the latest IDG Books catalog.